Cabinets and Built-Ins

H. H. Siegele

Sterling Publishing Co., Inc. New York
Oak Tree Press Co., Ltd. London & Sydney

Published in 1980 by
Sterling Publishing Co., Inc.
Two Park Avenue
New York, N.Y. 10016

ISBN 0-8069-8188-1

Previously
ISBN: 0-8473-1122-8

Printed in The United States Of America

PREFACE

The advent of plywood, as it is known today, has revolutionized cabinet and built-ins construction. The old fashioned kitchen built-ins and built-ons are not only out-of-date, but they are fast becoming out of use. For those householders who can afford it, are doing away with them to make room for cabinets and built-ins that more adequately serve the needs of our day. And it is hoped that the day is not far away, when all householders can have the satisfaction that goes with these modern facilities.

THE AUTHOR

CONTENTS

CABINETS AND BUILT-INS

Chapter 1

KITCHEN BUILT-INS

The advent of plywood has practically eliminated the old-style built-ins that required moldings and panelwork, especially panel doors. A house built today without the increased number of conveniences that up-to-date built-ins provide, could hardly be called modern.

Kitchen Built-Ins.—Fig. 1 gives a face view of a built-in kitchen cabinet in the rough. Here the rough frame and the shelves are shown. Fig. 2 shows the same layout with the doors

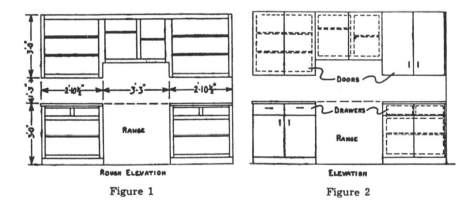

| Figure 1 | Figure 2 |

and drawers in place. The dotted lines upper left and bottom right, show the position of the rough frame and shelves of the cabinet — that is to say, the dotted lines show the relationship of the rough framework in Fig. 1, to the doors and the drawers after they are in place. The handles of the doors are indicated on the doors to the upper right and to the bottom left. Two drawer pulls are also shown. The hinges are practically concealed.

Cross Sections.—Fig. 3 shows, to the left, the left end view of the built-in case shown in the two previous figures. At the center is shown a cross section of the layout shown by Fig. 1.

Here it will be noticed that the doors and drawers have been
omitted. To the right we have a cross section of the layout shown
by Fig. 2. It will be seen that the doors and drawers are in
place here.

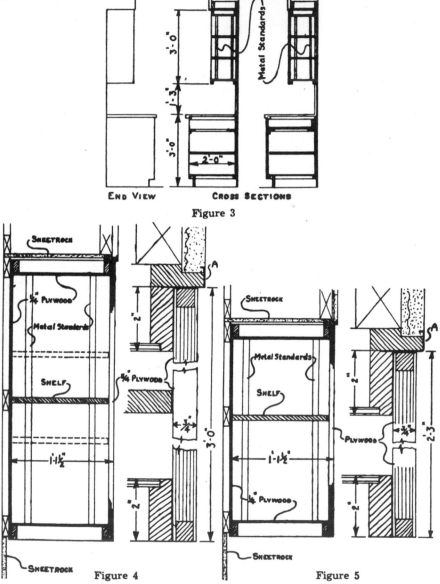

Figure 3

Figure 4   Figure 5

Details of Cases.—Fig. 4 shows to the left a cross section of the two large upper cases. A shelf is shown at the center. By the dotted lines a different arrangement of the shelves is shown. To the right are shown details of the construction and of the doors. At **A** is pointed out a metal binding. Fig. 5 shows to the left a cross section of the center case. This case is shorter than

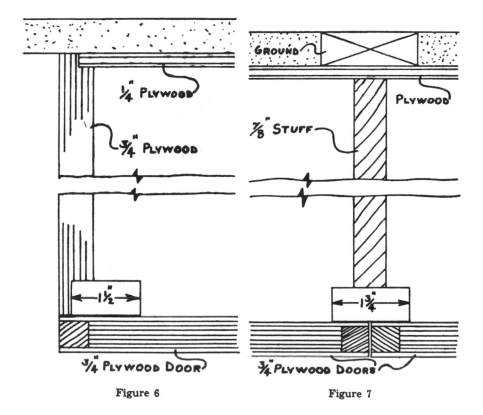

Figure 6   Figure 7

the other two and has only one shelf. The metal binding is again pointed out at **A**. The construction shown by the details is the same as in the other two cases.

Details showing sections of the construction are shown by Figs. 6, 7, and 8. Fig. 6 shows the construction of the left end of the cabinet. Quarter-inch plywood is used for the back, which is placed flat against the plaster. The end is made of three-quarter-inch plywood. The same thickness of plywood is used for the doors. Fig. 7 shows the center construction where the two doors meet. A plaster ground is shown here. Fig. 8 shows the construction of the right end of the case, where it joins the plastering. A one-inch style is scribed to the plastering. Study and compare the three details. Notice how the edges of the doors have been grooved and a strip of wood has been inserted and glued, as shown by the details. This gives the edges of the doors a much nicer finish, and also reinforces the doors.

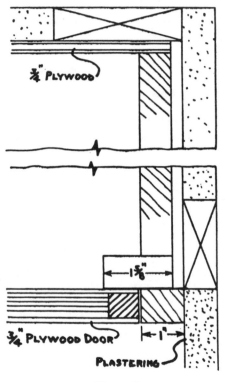

Figure 8

Rough Frame.—A joint of a rough upper corner of the rough frame is shown by Fig. 9. By dotted lines a mortise and tenon joint is indicated. This is a typical joint. Fig. 10 shows the same kind of joint for the upper left corner of the framework.

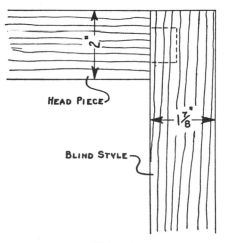

Figure 9

  The illustrations in this chapter should be kept in mind, for they cover much of the construction that will be used in other built-in cases.

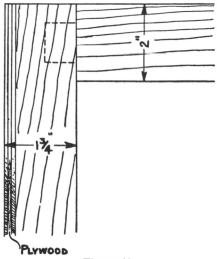

Figure 10

Chapter 2

HINGES AND DRAWERS

Power-Tool Efficiency.—Even though the time will never come when the field carpenter will take over making everything on a job without using mill-made fixtures, the time is here when he can do many things that not so long ago were thought to be impossible. The efficiency of power tools is responsible for this change. There are few things that go into a first class home, or a first class building of any kind, that can not be done right on the job. Of course, in many cases the ordinary carpenter, no matter how well be might be equipped with power tools, can not compete with the mills. But there are always some circumstances that will eliminate competition, and the man who is prepared for such instances will get the work. This is particularly true of built-in cabinets for homes. The man who has the power tools to do that kind of work, can get such little jobs finished without much, if any, delay.

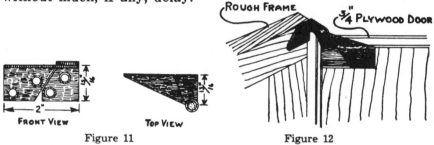

Figure 11   Figure 12

Concealed Hinges.—The doors of the built-in cabinets that were discussed in the last chapter and those covered in this chapter are hung with hinges that are almost completely concealed. Fig. 11, to the left, shows a front view of such a hinge. To the right a top view is shown. Fig. 12 shows a perspective view of the hinge fastened to the case and to the door. When the doors are hung and closed, only an edge view of the hinge swivels can be seen. The main parts of the hinges will be back of the doors.

Cross Sections.—Fig. 13 shows a cross section of the bottom cases of the built-in cabinets shown by Figs. 1 and 2. The draw-

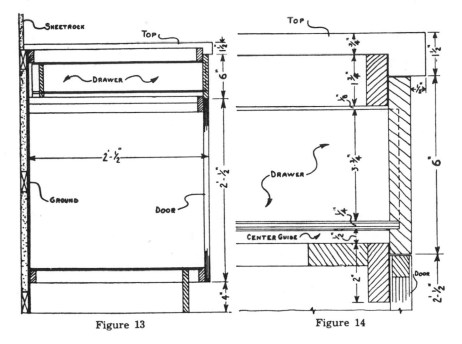

Figure 13   Figure 14

ing shows the sheetrock that is used on the wall between the upper and the bottom cases. The top is pointed out. The owner must decide on the kind of top he wants, because he will have

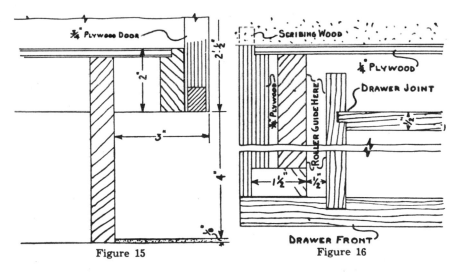

Figure 15   Figure 16

to pay the bill. The drawer, a ground, and the door are also pointed out. A detail of the top and the drawer, in part, are shown by Fig. 14. The different dimensions are given in figures. At the bottom of the detail, the top of the door is shown. Fig. 15 gives a detail of the bottom construction of the front. The

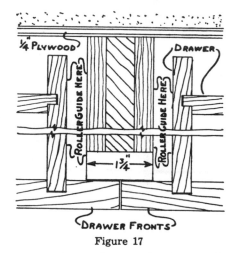

Figure 17

bottom of the door is pointed out here. Study Figs. 14 and 15 along with Fig. 13.

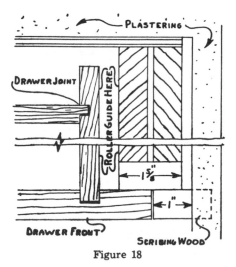

Figure 18

Drawer Details.—Fig. 16 shows, in plan, a section of the left side of a drawer, in part, together with the left side of the case for the drawer. Much of the case and of the drawer is not shown. By dotted lines the allowance for scribing is indicated.

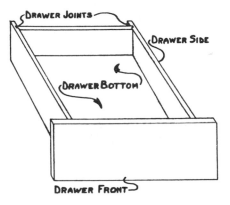

Figure 19

The quarter-inch plywood back, the three-quarter-inch plywood end, and the drawer front are also pointed out. Fig. 17 is a detail showing the construction of the case between two drawers and the parts of the two drawers in their right relationship to the case. These drawers are equipped with roller guides, which

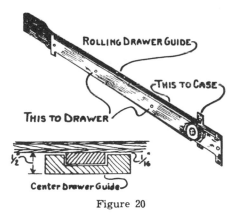

Figure 20

come in two parts. One of the parts is fastened to the drawer and the other to the frame. Fig. 18 shows details of the right side of the case and parts of the drawer. By dotted lines the allowance for scribing is shown. It should be remembered that these details show sections of the case and the parts of the drawers cut horizontally, or on a level.

Drawer and Drawer Guide.—Fig. 19 shows a perspective view of a drawer. The joints, drawer side, drawer bottom, and drawer front are pointed out. Fig. 20 is a drawing of the roller drawer guide that is used on the cabinets we are dealing with here. This figure, to the bottom left, shows a center guide, used on all drawers. Fig. 21 is a perspective view of a kitchen layout, in which the style of construction, shown in this chapter is used.

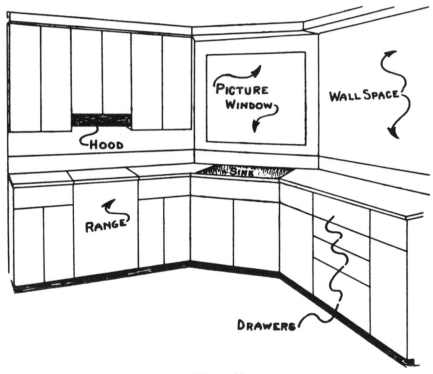

Figure 21

Chapter 3

PLAN OF KITCHEN AND CABINETS

Kitchen Cabinets.—The kitchen is a leading part of any home. In many respects it is the principal room of the house. Here is where the food is prepared for the table, and the way this is done has a lot to do with the happiness of the family. For cleanliness, the room should be well lighted, either with natural light, or with the right kind of artificial light. The cabinets should be conveniently arranged. This can not be acomplished without the cooperation and approval of the person or persons that will be using it.

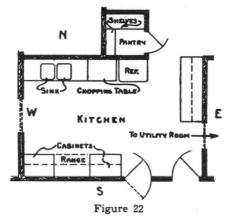

Figure 22

The Kitchen.—Fig. 22 is a drawing of the kitchen that was used as a basis for these first three chapters. The arrangements of the other parts of the house had something to do with the arrangement that is shown on the drawing. This should be remembered, in case it is used for a basis in planning other kitchens. The sink, the chopping or work table, the refrigerator, and the pantry are shown on the north of the room. The range and cabinets are on the south wall, while the east wall has a door to the utility room and cabinets for linens.

Linen Cabinets.—Fig. 23 shows the elevation of the east wall of the kitchen shown by Fig. 22. Section **A-A** is shown to the left drawn to a larger scale. The poles that are pointed out are used for tablecloths. Fig. 24 is a perspective view of the pole drawer, which has no bottom. The tablecloths are hung over the poles, and the drawer can be pulled out and pushed back.

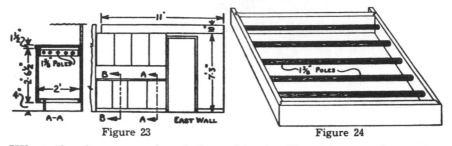

Figure 23   Figure 24

When the doors are closed the cabinet will appear as shown in the elevation, Fig. 23. Fig. 25 shows a smaller pole drawer that is used for holding towels. To the left is shown a small

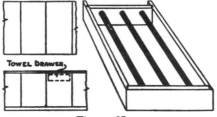

Figure 25

scale elevation, in part, of cabinets showing by dotted lines the location of the drawer. As many of these drawers as are needed should be provided. The elevation shows how the cabinet will

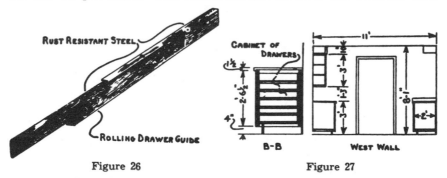

Figure 26   Figure 27

appear when the doors are closed. Fig. 26 gives a drawing of a rolling drawer guide suitable for the drawers just discussed.

West Wall.—To the right in Fig. 27 is show an elevation of the west wall. Section **B-B**, to the left, is a cross section of a linen cabinet shown by Fig. 23 in elevation. The drawing is placed here in order to conserve space. Fig. 28 gives a perspective view of one of the drawers shown in section **B-B**. Notice the cut-out part. The purpose of this is twofold: It provides a drawer pull, and at the same time makes it possible to look into the drawer without pulling it out. For instance, you open the door, and at a glance you can tell which drawer holds the article or articles you want.

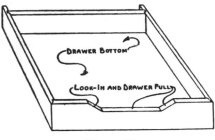

Figure 28

North Wall.—The north wall is shown by Fig. 29. To the left is shown a large three-light window of plate glass. This provides ample light for the kitchen sink and the work or chopping table. The refrigerator is conveniently located next to the chopping table. By referring to Fig. 22, you will notice that the pantry is not far from the refrigerator. Section **C-C**, Fig. 30, is a cross section through **C-C**, Fig. 29. Here the construction of

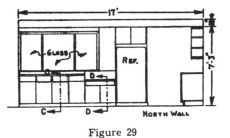

Figure 29

the case is shown, excepting the part that supports the sink. This is left out so that the owner can select a sink that will suit his own needs. The framework for supporting the sink must be worked out accordingly. Fig. 31 shows a cross section of the work or chopping table through **D-D,** Fig. 29. The top **of the** chopping table is made of 1″ x 2″ strips of oak or maple, **glued** together.

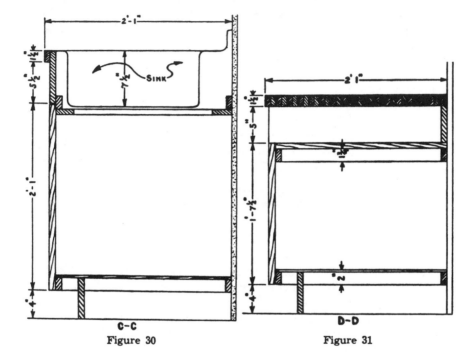

C-C

Figure 30

D-D

Figure 31

South Wall.—An elevation of the south wall is **shown by** Fig. 32. The cases shown here were covered quite **thoroughly**

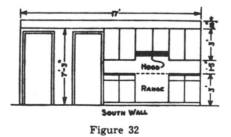

Figure 32

in chapter 1. The student should refer to this chapter **and study** this drawing in keeping with what he finds there.

Chapter 4

PLAN OF UTILITIES ROOM AND FIXTURES

Utility Room.—This room serves a great many purposes, especially in homes with limited floor space. In many instances, it is a storeroom for odds and ends, where you will find many things that otherwise would be in the kitchen. It is also the laundry, where the family washing and ironing is done. In some homes it is a sort of heating plant, for quite often the heating system is located in this room, especially the water heater. While it is not exactly a catch-all room, it often happens that it almost fills the requirements for such a room. Fig. 33 is a floor plan of the utility room that is used here as a basis for the discussions. This room exists, and is in use today.

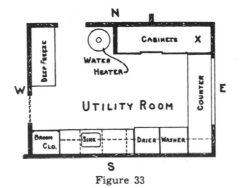

Figure 33

North Wall.—In Fig. 33 you will find that along the north wall are located, to the left, a deep freeze, joining the wall with one of its ends; a water heater, and cabinets with sliding doors. The location marked **X** should be kept in mind. Fig. 34 gives an elevation of the north wall. The incline of the ceiling line is the same as the incline of the roof, for the house is a ranch style house. Compare this elevation with the north part of the floor plan

Sliding Doors.—Fig. 35 shows in plan at the bottom, a small scale drawing of the sliding doors, pointed out in Fig. 34. The upper drawing gives the details of the same sliding doors. Details of the top and bottom of these sliding doors are shown

23

by Fig. 36. The symbols of hangers should be noticed. The doors are made of 1⅛-inch plywood, with the edges reinforced

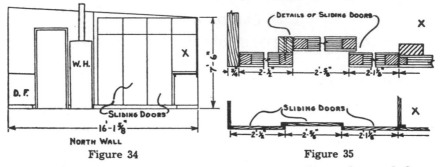

Figure 34   Figure 35

with an inserted strip of wood, just as all other plywood doors shown in these chapters are reinforced. Notice the grooves for the guides at the bottom.

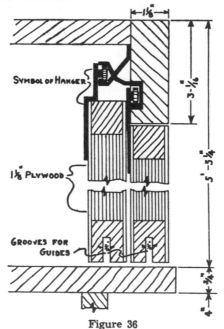

Figure 36

Cross Sections.—Fig. 37 shows to the left, a cross section through the sliding doors of the cabinet built against the north wall, Figs. 33 and 34. To the right over **X,** is a cross section of the cabinet that is marked **X** in Figs. 33, 34, and 35. Compare and study these in connection with the cross section over **X** in Fig. 37. The counter joins this part of the case, access to which is by means of the sliding doors. Notice the shelving above, and the standards that support them.

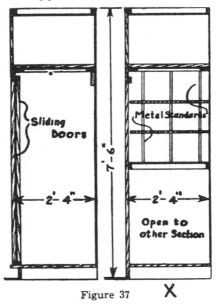

Figure 37   **X**

East Wall.—The east elevation of the utility room is shown in Fig. 38. To the extreme left is shown, in a larger scale, a cross section of the cases, cut through the elevation at **M-M** and **M-M**.

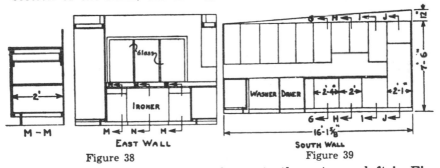

EAST WALL

Figure 38

SOUTH WALL

Figure 39

The case cut through **N-N**, is shown to the extreme left in Fig. 43. This part is open and used for storing the ironer. On the floor plan, Fig. 33, it is under the counter. Study the three drawings dealing with this part of the case.

South Wall.—An elevation of the south wall is shown by Fig. 39. Notice the ceiling here inclines the same as the one shown by the north elevation in Fig. 34. To the left is shown a cross section of the counter shown in Fig. 33. To the right of it is shown the washer, and then the drier. Section **G-G** is shown to the left in Fig. 40. The bottom part of this cabinet is used for holding soiled laundry. Section **H-H** is shown to the right in Fig. 40, giving a cross section of the sink. Fig. 41, to the left, shows section **I-I**, where the bottom part of the cabinet is equipped with drawers. The broom closet, section **J-J**, is shown to the right in Fig. 41. Locate this closet on the floor plan in Fig. 33.

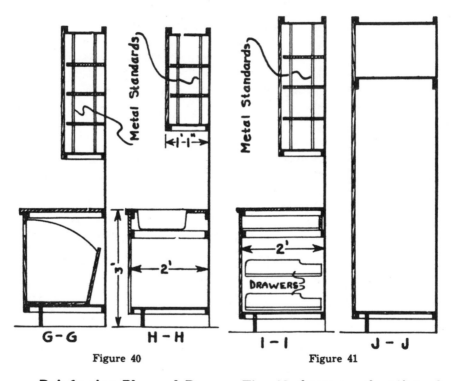

Figure 40   Figure 41

Reinforcing Plywood Doors.—Fig. 42 shows an elevation of a 2′ by 2′ 6″ plywood door. The dotted lines indicate the depth of the wood reinforcing on the edges of the door. At **A,** inset, is shown a cross section of one edge of the door, showing the wood reinforcing. At **B,** a mitered corner of the reinforcing is shown with the layer of veneer removed. All of the doors in this series of lessons dealing with built-in cabinets have the edges reinforced in this way.

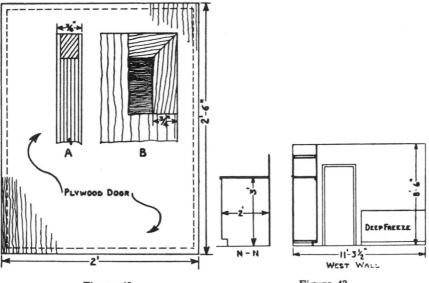

Figure 42   Figure 43

West Wall.—Fig. 43 shows the west wall elevation of the utility room. A cross section of the broom closet is shown to the left of the elevation, while to the right is shown the location of the deep freeze. Section **N-N**, to the extreme left, is shown in the east wall elevation, Fig. 38.

It should be remembered that in order to prevent confusion by too many notes, and due to limitations in space, it is expected that the student will read many things between the lines, especially with regard to matters that were covered in previous chapters. The general construction of the built-in cabinets of this work is the same, and after a construction has been covered by details, the student should, if he does not remember it, refer back to the chapter where it was covered.

Chapter 5

CLOSETS FOR BEDROOMS

Closets.—No house can have too many well-placed and well-planned closets. That is to say, that the closets will have to be conveniently located in the house, especially in the rooms. They should be planned in such a way that they will give the accommodations that are desired and needed by the occupants of the individual rooms. Bedroom closets should be provided with plenty of hook space, rods for hangers, shelf room, and drawer conveniences. These facilities should be selected to satisfy the wants and needs of the person or persons that are the most likely to occupy the different rooms. This means that teenagers should have the accommodations that such youngsters like to have in a room. In this connection, it must be remembered that boys and girls do not like or want the same things. The same is true of grown-ups. Where the room is occupied by couples, the closet should be made to accommodate both the woman and the man. Guest rooms need expert attention.

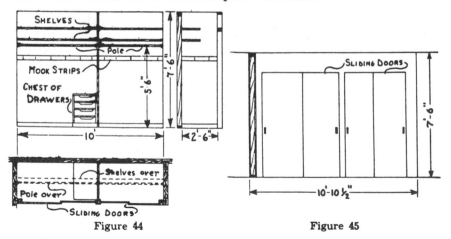

Figure 44

Figure 45

Bedroom Closet.—Fig. 44 shows at the bottom a floor plan of a bedroom closet. The back wall with shelves, poles, and hook strips is shown above. To the right is shown one of the end walls. The other end wall matches the one shown. A chest of drawers is shown to the left of the center partition, details of which will be taken up in another part of this chapter. Fig. 45 shows a front elevation of the closet, showing two sets of sliding doors in a closed position.

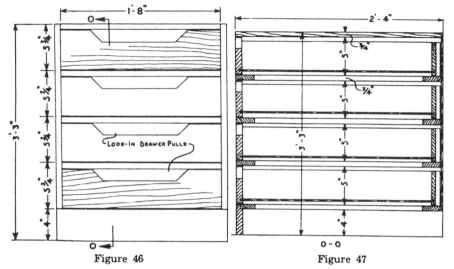

Figure 46 Figure 47

Look-In Drawers.—Fig. 46 is a face view of the chest of drawers, giving the various dimensions in figures. The openings serve a twofold purpose: First, they make it possible to look into

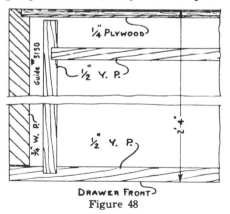

DRAWER FRONT
Figure 48

the drawers and find the drawer that holds the article or articles that you want, before pulling the drawer out; and second, they make excellent drawer pulls. The arrows at **O-O** show where the case is cut, as shown in cross section in **Fig. 47**. Here the construction of the drawers and the case can be studied in keeping with the larger scale details.

Details of Construction.—Fig. 48 shows in two parts, the front and back constructions of the drawer, cut horizontally. Notice the space allowed for the roller guides. Figs. 49 and 50 should be studied in keeping with the center guide shown in part in Fig. 51. This drawing shows the left half of the face of the drawer in parts. One half of the center guide, already referred to, is shown to the right. The face board of the front is cut out here to give a cross section of the guide. The upper strip (hard wood) is glued to the drawer bottom. The grooved part is fastened to the frame directly under the drawer. This detail shows the bottom drawer and the base of the case, in parts.

Shelves and Drawers.—Fig. 52 shows at the bottom a plan

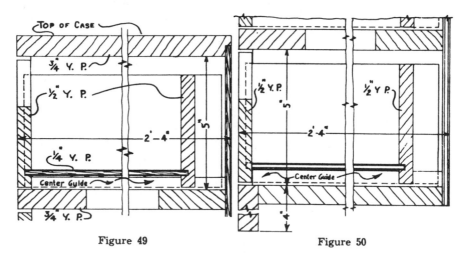

Figure 49   Figure 50

of a closet with shelves and a chest of drawers. These drawers are larger than the drawers just explained. The look-in windows are much larger, making it possible to inspect the contents quite thoroughly before pulling out the drawer. The construction of these drawers are exactly the same as those that were illustrated and explained in the foregone paragraphs, excepting that the face board is made of ¾-inch stuff. A face view of the shelves and drawers are shown by the main drawing above. To the right of the main drawing is shown a cross section of the shelves. The floor plan shows the sliding doors.

Smaller Closets.—At the center and right of Fig. 53 are shown, respectively, the back wall and the right wall of this closet. At the bottom, center, we have a floor plan. The drawers shown are without windows, but the construction is the same

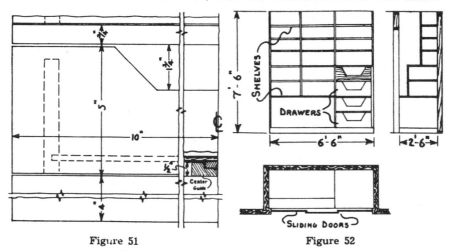

Figure 51   Figure 52

as the construction explained in the first part of this chapter. The face boards can be either ½-inch or ¾-inch stuff. To the left, at the bottom, is shown a floor plan of a very small closet, which is equipped with a shelf, hook strips, and a rod for

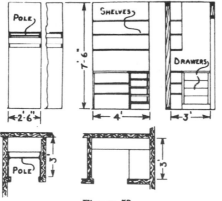

Figure 53

hangers. Above the plan is shown the back wall, and to the right a part of one of the side walls, which shows the hook strips and shelf.

Chapter 6

SHOWER, BATHROOM AND FIXTURES

The Bathroom.—A most important room of any house is the bathroom. It should be as up-to-date as the means of the owner will permit. Sanitation, comfort, and convenience are cardinal requirements of any bathroom. Implied in the three are hot and cold water, proper means of cleanliness, careful and correct arrangements, and well controlled and well measured temperatures. These all belong to first requisites. After that can be added luxuries, such as persons of means can afford. If the means are great the luxuries can be of the most expensive types, while those of more modest means will have to govern the luxuries according to what their means will justify, or their judgments will dictate.

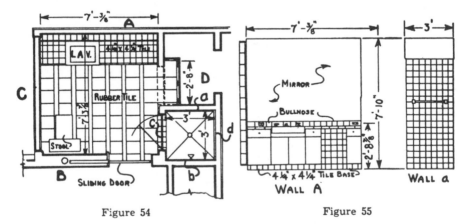

Figure 54   Figure 55

Bathroom Floor Plan.—Fig. 54 shows a floor plan of a bathroom with shower bath closet. The four walls of the main room are indicated by capital letters, **A, B, C,** and **D,** while the walls of the shower closet are indicated by the small letters, **a, b, c,** and **d.** The dimensions of the main room and the closet are shown on the drawing.

Elevations of Walls.—Fig. 55 shows elevations of wall **A** of the main room, and wall **a** of the shower closet. Notice the large mirror and the absence of the medicine chest above the lavatory. Instead you will find built-in cabinets with doors and drawers, directly under the tiled counter top. The tile, both in the main and in the minor drawings, should be kept in mind. The latter shows the location of a towel bar. Elevations of walls

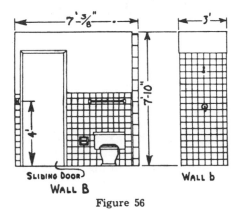

SLIDING DOOR
WALL B

WALL b

Figure 56

B and **b** are shown by Fig. 56. The main drawing shows the sliding door, the stool, a towel bar, and a paper holding fixture. Wall **b** of the shower, shows the location of the sprinklers. Fig. 57 shows the elevation of walls **C** and **c**. The dimensions of

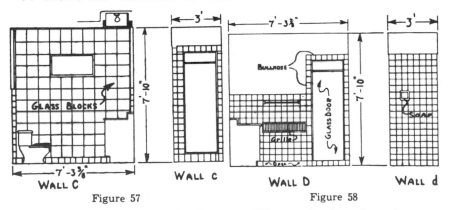

GLASS BLOCKS

WALL C

WALL c

BULLNOSE

GLASS DOOR

GRILLE

WALL D

SOAP

WALL d

Figure 57   Figure 58

these walls are given in figures. The main drawing shows a side view of the stool, a cross section of the lavatory counter, and a small window. This wall is finished with glass blocks. Wall **c** shows the door with a transom to the shower closet. Fig. 58 shows elevations of walls **D** and **d**. The main drawing shows the glass door to the shower, while wall **d** shows a soap holder together with the tile finish of the wall.

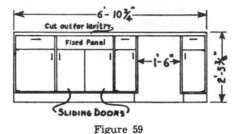

Figure 59

Built-In Cabinets.—Fig. 59 shows a face view of the built-in cabinets under the lavatory counter. Two sliding doors are pointed out directly under the fixed panel. The space directly back of the fixed panel is to be utilized by the lavatory. Notice the open section toward the right — also the drawers and cabinet doors. The drawers take the place of the old-style medicine chest.

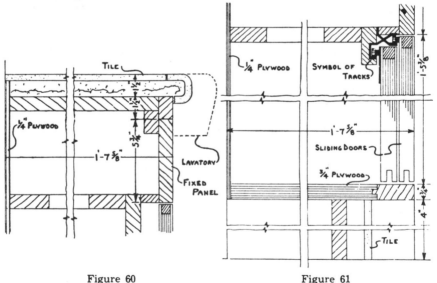

Figure 60   Figure 61

Details of Construction.—Cross section details, giving the construction of the case with the tile top in place, are shown by Fig. 60. An outline of a lavatory nosing is shown by dotted lines. The lavatory part is left indefinite, so that the owner can choose a lavatory that will satisfy his likes and needs. Fig. 61 shows cross section details of the case directly under what is shown by Fig. 60. Here the sliding doors are pointed out. Notice the symbol of tracks for the sliding doors. There are tracks on the market somewhat like the symbols on the drawing, however,

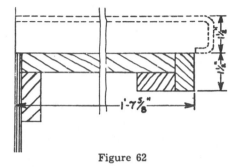

Figure 62

there are other good tracks that can be used, therefore symbols of tracks are shown. The grooves shown in the bottom edges of the sliding doors are for the guides of the doors. Study this drawing with the one shown by Fig. 60, where the symbol is omitted. The two drawings constitute the lavatory part of the

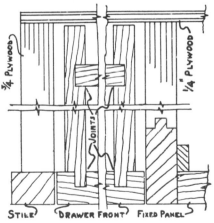

Figure 63

cabinet. Fig. 62 shows cross section details of the top over the open part of the lavatory cabinet. The relationship of the tile top to the wooden part is indicated by the dotted lines above, and gives the location of the tile top, which must be bedded in cement.

Drawers.—Fig. 63 shows in plan, a section through the drawer shown to the left in Fig. 59 and also in Fig. 55. Much of the construction of the drawers and the wooden part of the cabinet is like what has been shown in previous chapters. For this reason it should be studied with the other constructions in mind. Pointed out on the drawing are the plywood parts, the

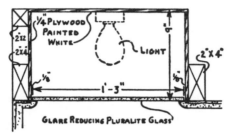

Figure 64

joints, the stile that joins the wall, the drawer front, and the fixed panel. Fig. 64 shows a larger scale drawing of the concealed light, giving the size in figures. A glare reducing pluralite glass, as pointed out, hides the light bulb.

Chapter 7

PRINCIPAL BATHROOM

Details Bathroom Doors.—Details of the sliding door, shown by Figs. 54 and 56, are given here in Figs. 65 and 66. The upper part of Fig. 65 shows the construction of the head of the door opening. Also the tracks and the finishing. The hangers are not shown. The bottom part shows how the door joins the floor over

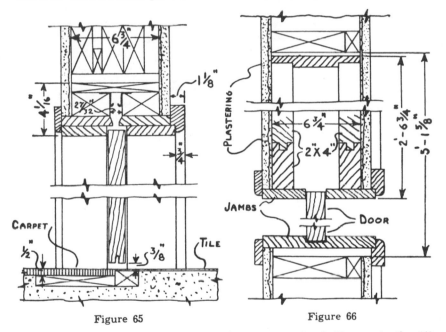

Figure 65   Figure 66

the point where the carpet, pointed out to the left, meets the tile of the bathroom floor. The two parts of the drawing, also show the top and bottom part of the sliding door. Fig. 66 shows the construction of the jambs, both rough and finish. The upper parts show how the pocket, into which the door slides, is constructed. The bottom drawing shows the side jamb with the groove that receives the door when it is closed. The size of the opening and the pocket can be figured out by the figures given.

It is expected that the student will read some things between the lines. This is important, for if everything is pointed out, the reader could easily be tempted to omit studying the drawings.

Tile Top of Cabinets.—Fig. 67 is a drawing giving a cross section outline of the cabinet. The purpose of this figure is to give the construction of the tile tops of the two cabinets. The tile are bedded in cement, reinforced with metal lath. The

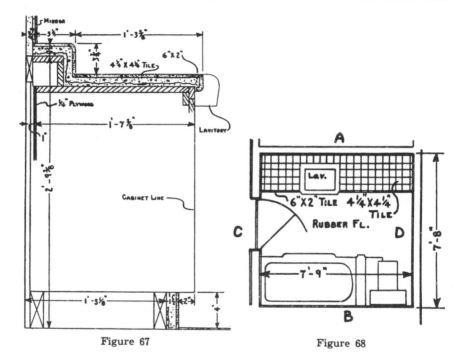

Figure 67   Figure 68

irregular line indicates metal lath. A part of the mirror is pointed out at the upper left. Notice the nosing part of the lavatory.

Floor Plan and Walls.—In the last chapter a floor plan was shown of the bathroom with a shower closet. The floor plan shown here Fig. 68 is of a bathroom with a tub. The four walls are indicated by the letters **A, B, C,** and **D.** The size of the room is given by figures. Fig. 69 is an elevation of wall **A.** Here the mirror is pointed out, and the front of the cabinet is given. Another drawing of the cabinet is shown by Fig. 70, where the sliding doors are pointed out, also the part of the cabinet that is to be cut out for the lavatory. The lavatory must be installed, before the tile top is put on. See Fig. 67 for a cross section of the tile top. The construction of the drawers and other parts of this cabinet were covered in the previous chapter.

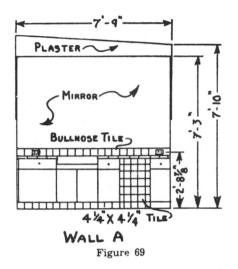

WALL A

Figure 69

An elevation of wall **B** is shown by Fig. 71. Here the plastered wall, the bullnose finish of the wainscoting, and the tub are pointed out. An end view of the partition between the tub and the stool is shown here, shaded. Fig. 72 shows to the left a cross section of the wainscoting, part of which is cut out. The figures give the exact height. The center drawing gives the end view of the partition between the tub and the stool, already

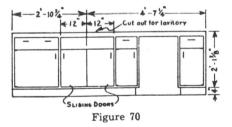

Figure 70

referred to. To the right we have a cross section, showing the relationship of the partition to the tub. Notice how the tile of both the wainscoting and the partition are bedded in reinforced cement. The irregular lines indicate metal lath.

Wall **C**, Fig. 73, shows an end view of the tub, the wainscoting, the door opening, and to the right a cross section of the

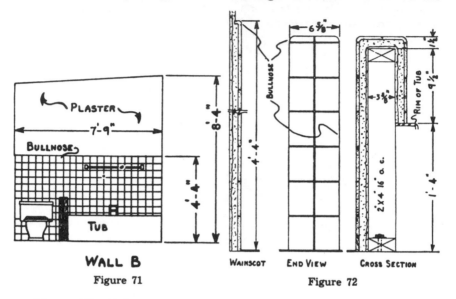

WALL B

Figure 71

WAINSCOT   END VIEW   CROSS SECTION

Figure 72

cabinet. The light fixture shown to the upper right, will be taken up by detail in the next chapter. Fig. 74 shows a detail of one

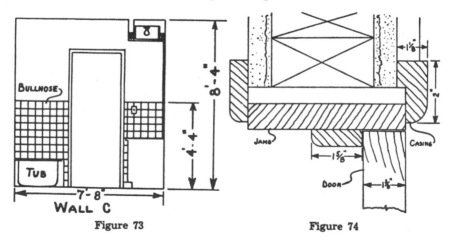

WALL C

Figure 73

Figure 74

side of the door jamb. The other side and head of the jamb are constructed practically like the detail shown. The part of the door, the door stop, the jamb, and the casings are shown by this figure in a rather large scale.

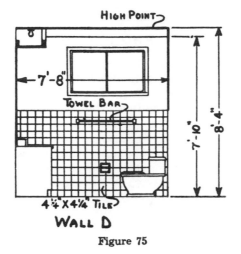

WALL D

Figure 75

An elevation of wall **D** is given by Fig. 75. Here the tile wainscoting is shown, a cross section of the cabinet, a paper holder, the stool, and a towel bar. The figures to the right give the high and low points of the ceiling. The reason for this is that the ceiling of the room, inclines the same as the roof. This is also shown by Figs. 69 and 71. The ceilings of the ranch-style house with two bathrooms follows the incline in keeping with the slope of the roof.

Chapter 8

LIGHT AND SHELVING

Concealed Lights.—Fig. 76 is a holdover from the last chapter. It shows a detail of a concealed light. The glare reducing pluralite glass should be noted. This glass conceals the light bulb, and at the same time reduces the glare. It is a step forward in lighting, but it is not the last word in that field. Constant improvements are being made, and no doubt will continue to be made, in the direction of perfection. Whether we are approaching the advent of perfect artificial lighting, is difficult to say. The thing that is certain, is that we are constantly advancing, and probably will continue to do so. But perfection is something

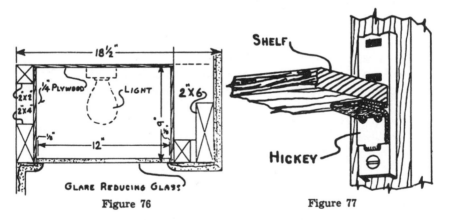

Figure 76   Figure 77

that still exists only in the realm of idealism. In the field of realities, we must content ourselves with constant improvements.

Hickey Supports.—A shelf-supporting hickey is shown by Fig. 77. In this case a metal channel with adjusting slots every half inch, is fastened to the wooden standard with screws, as shown by the drawing. These slots make possible ½-inch shelf adjustments. Fig. 78 shows the same kind of metal channel with slots, set into a groove in the standard, as shown by the drawing. In this case a different hickey is shown. This shelf support also provides for ½-inch shelf adjustments. Another standard for supporting shelves is shown by Fig. 79. This has a

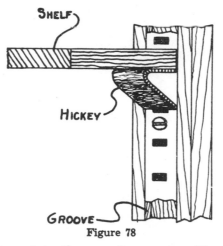

Figure 78

metal strip fastened to the wooden part, with slots every half inch. Two kinds of hickeys are shown here. The metal strip is fastened to the wooden standard with screws.

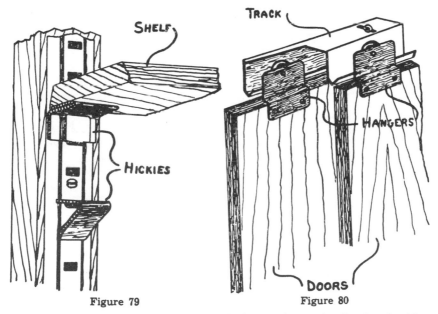

Figure 79 Figure 80

Tracks and Hangers.—Fig. 80 shows, in parts, the back sides of two sliding doors. The hangers in this instance are fastened to the back of the doors, which hides them from the front view. Fig. 81 gives a cross section of a double track, two doors in parts, and the roller hangers. The bottom edges of the doors have grooves for guides. These are light sliding doors, such as are shown by the drawings of the bathroom cabinets in the last

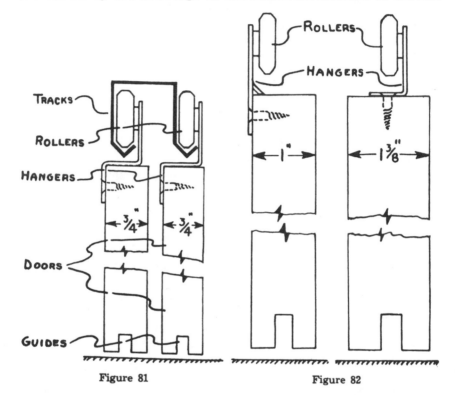

Figure 81   Figure 82

two chapters. The front of the doors is to the right. Fig. 82 shows to the left a cross section in parts, of a 1-inch door, with a straight roller hanger fastened to the back of the door at the top. To the right is shown a cross section of a 1⅜-inch door, with a roller hanger that is fastened to the top edge of the door. Notice the grooves at the bottom that guide the bottom of the doors.

Single Tracks.—Two single tracks are shown by Fig. 83. The one to the left has a flange at the top by which it is fastened to the header of the opening. This track is used principally for doors that slide into pockets. The track to the right is suit-

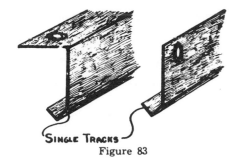

SINGLE TRACKS
Figure 83

able for sliding doors of show cases, and the like.

Drawer Guides.—Fig. 84 gives a drawing of one-half of a set of drawer guides for kitchen cabinets. These guides come

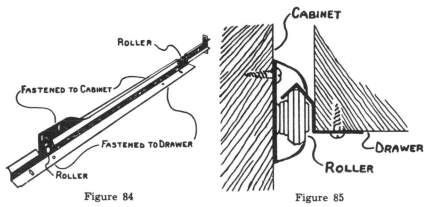

Figure 84   Figure 85

in two parts. One part is fastened to the cabinet and the other part is screwed on the bottom of the drawer. Enough of the metal frame is shown cut out, to reveal the two rollers. The roller pointed out at the upper right is attached to the part of the frame that is fastened to the drawer, while the roller shown to the left is on the other part of the frame. Fig. 85 gives a cross section diagram, showing the two parts in position. A little study of this diagram will reveal the fact that the track that is fastened to the bottom of the drawer, rides the roller pointed out to the left in Fig. 84. The roller shown to the right runs on a track.

In general terms, it is suggested that working drawings be secured from the manufacturers of whatever kind of hardware that might be used, not only in cabinet work, but in any other kind of finishing that requires such hardware.

Chapter 9

KITCHEN CABINETS

Old Kitchens.—Here is a wide and fertile field for the carpenter who has a set of well-chosen power tools. There are a great many homes that still have the old fashioned kitchens.

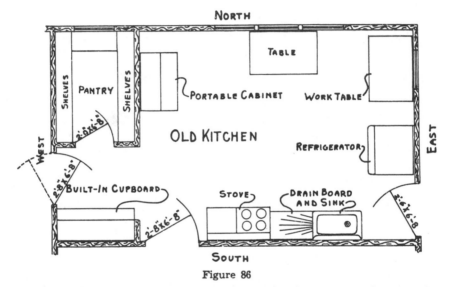

Figure 86

Many of these kitchens will be modernized sooner or later. The workman who is prepared to do this kind of work well, and by advertising, can convince owners of such out-of-date kitchens, that they should be remodeled, will be on the road to a business of his own. For instance, in the block where this writer lives, within the last two years, three old kitchens have been modernized. One of those kitchens is the one that is shown in Fig. 86, as it was. Fig. 87 shows how it was changed into a modern kitchen.

West Wall.—Fig. 88 gives a drawing of the west wall of the kitchen, as shown by Fig. 87. The wainscoting is made of 4¼″ x 4¼″ tile. Fig. 89 shows a section through **A-A**. To the right is shown a cross section, giving the construction of a desk, which we will call the housewife's desk. In this desk she can keep pencil, paper, recipes, cook book, telephone directory, and many other little things that she wants to keep in a con-

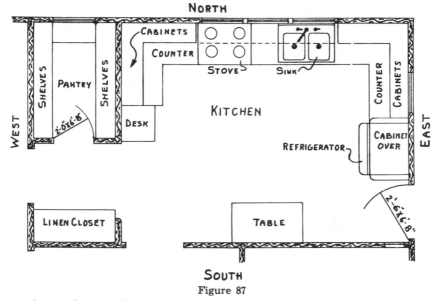

Figure 87

venient place. The desk topping is pointed out. In this case Formica was used, but there are different kinds of materials that

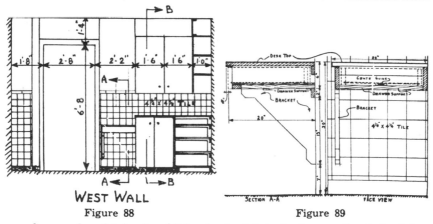

WEST WALL
Figure 88

Figure 89

can be used, which should be looked into before a final decision is made. Perhaps the best material to use for supporting the topping, is ¾-inch plywood. Here again, the designer should take into consideration materials that are available, and choose, if the choice is left to him, the materials that will give the best

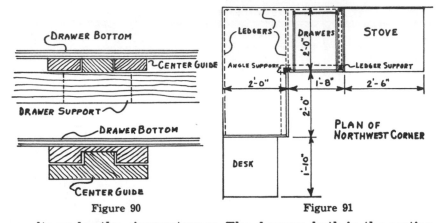

Figure 90

Figure 91

results under the circumstances. The drawer, both in the section to the left and in the face view to the right, is indicated by

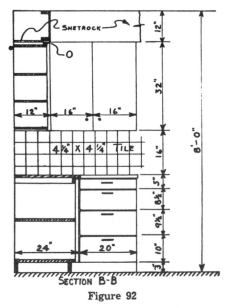

Figure 92

dotted lines. The bracket is cut out of ¾-inch plywood. Only one bracket is needed, since one side of the desk is joined to the counter, which supports it. The height of the desk is 30

inches, as shown by figures between the two views. The center
guide is pointed out on the face view.

Details of Center Guides.—Fig. 90 shows two designs of
center guides. The strips to the right and to the left, on the
upper drawing, are fastened to the bottom of the drawer with
glue and small brads. The center piece is fastened to the drawer
support, also with glue and brads. The bottom drawing shows
a tongue and groove center guide.

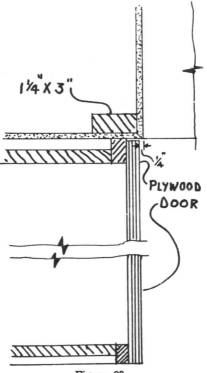

1¼" X 3"

PLYWOOD
DOOR

¼"

Figure 93

Plan of Northwest Corner.—The plan shown by Fig. 91 is
of the northwest corner of the pattern kitchen. Here we show
the desk and counter that join the west wall. The drawers and
stove that are shown in this drawing, join the north wall. Ledgers that support the counter top are indicated by dotted lines.

Section B-B.—Fig. 92 shows the construction of the dropped
ceiling above the cabinets and also the construction of the cab-

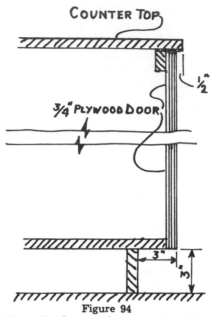

Figure 94

inet. At the bottom it shows the construction of the counter. A face view of the dropped ceiling, cabinets, wainscoting, and the drawers, that join the north wall toward the west end, are shown here in elevation. Fig. 93 is a detail of the construction

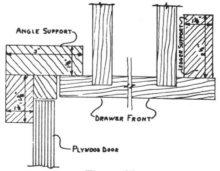

Figure 95

where the cases join the dropped ceiling, particularly at point **O**. Fig. 94 shows a similar detail of the counter. Fig. 95 gives in detail the construction of the angle support and the ledger support, showing the relationship of them to the drawers. To the left the plywood door, in part, is shown.

Chapter 10

LINEN CLOSET

Linen Closet.—A linen closet, built-in or otherwise, is a necessity in any modern home. Such a closet can be built into a wall, or it can be built onto a wall, depending to a great extent on existing circumstances.

Fig. 96 shows, at the bottom, a plan of a simple linen closet.

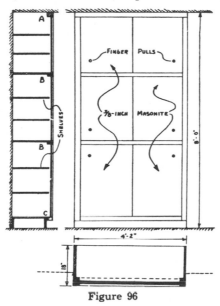

Figure 96

The dotted lines, one to the left and one to the right, show how such a closet can be built into a wall, with part of the cabinet extending out from the wall, as those lines indicate. The dotted line shown toward the front on the plan, indicates the inside edges of the grooved sills—the two that separate the three sections, and the one at the bottom. More will be said on this when the details are taken up. Shelves, finger pulls, and the masonite sliding doors are pointed out on the two upper drawings. To the left we have a cross section, and to the right an elevation of the cabinet. Three dimensions, of this cabinet, are shown in

51

figures. The assumption here is that the shelves are housed into the side pieces of the cabinet.

Details of Cabinets.—Two parts of a cabinet similar to the one shown in Fig. 96, are shown in Fig. 97. These drawings show a much better design than what is shown by the previous drawings. Here only the four principal shelves are housed into the side pieces, while the rest of the shelves are supported by metal standards, indicating that these shelves are adjustable.

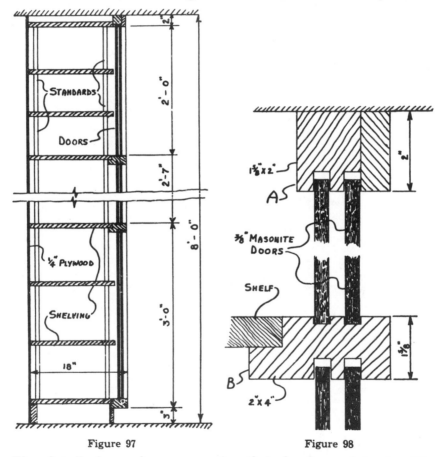

Figure 97　　　　　　　　　Figure 98

The details here show a one-fourth-inch plywood back. The purpose in showing different constructions, is to give the workman, or student, a chance to make a decision as to what construction will take care of the existing needs the best.

Fig. 98 shows details of the top rail, marked **A**, and the sills, marked **B**, in this figure. How the top rail and the sills are

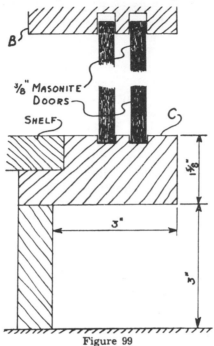

Figure 99

grooved for the sliding doors is shown here. The ⅜-inch masonite doors in parts, are also shown. Notice that the grooves for

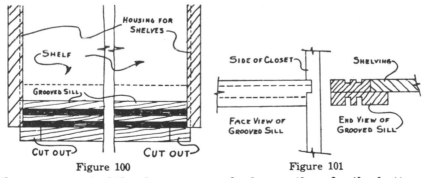

Figure 100   Figure 101

the upper part of the doors are made deeper than for the bottom part, so that the doors can be slipped up enough to let them into place easily—in other words, so that the doors can be put into place and taken out without difficulty. Study the drawings. Fig. 99 shows the construction of the toe-room at the bottom of the cabinet, and the bottom sill, marked **C** here and in Fig. 96—it also shows the relationship of the doors to the sills marked **B.** How the stationary shelves join the sills should be noted.

The details given by Fig. 100 show how the shelves and the grooved sills are housed into the sides of the cabinet. The depth of the housing is indicated by dotted lines. How the grooved sills are cut out for the casings, is shown by the "cut out" indicators. The horizontal dotted line, indicates the back edge of the grooved sill, where it is rabbeted to receive the shelving. See Fig. 101, where to the left, a face view of a grooved sill is shown, joined to a side piece. To the right we have an end view of the sill and shelving, before they are joined to the side piece. Fig. 102 shows the layout shown by Fig. 100, after the jambs and casings were put in place. The student should study the relationship of the different drawings carefully.

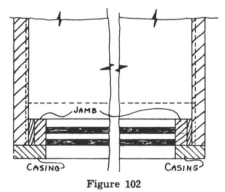

Figure 102

Different Method.—Fig. 103 shows, perhaps a better method of holding the sliding doors in place, although it will require more work to do the job. In this method the bottom edge of the door has a small tongue worked on it, as shown by the upper part of the drawing, while the upper part of the door has a longer tongue worked onto it, as shown by the bottom part of the drawing. The advantage in this way of installing sliding doors, is that the doors can be held much closer together, as a comparison of Fig. 98 with Fig. 103 reveal. The appearance, also will be better.

Finger Pulls.—Fig. 104 gives a full-size drawing of a finger pull, such as are commonly used on sliding cabinet doors. At

A is shown a hole bored in the door to receive the finger pull, while at **B** we have a cross section of the same hole. At **C** is shown a face view of the finger pull in place, and at **D** we have a cross section of the same pull in place.

Play and Smoothness.—A word should be said here about the matter of making sliding doors of cabinets work smoothly. There are several ways to do this. First, the groove should be made as smooth as possible. Second, there should be ample play for the door when in place, but at the same time not too much. Third, the grooves and the contact edges of the sliding

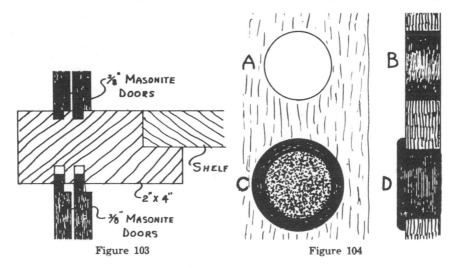

Figure 103   Figure 104

doors should have a thorough treatment of wax. Parafin wax is often used, and gives good results. A good quality of floor wax will also give excellent results. Whatever will add smoothness to the door when it is used is all right. Fourth, avoid any material for the doors that will warp in seasoning to the extent that it will cause enough friction in the grooves so as to become obstructive to smoothness in the operation of the doors.

Chapter 11

ELEVATION AND DETAILS

Built-Ins.—One of the first considerations of those who are looking for a home, to build, to buy, or to rent, is built-ins. The old built-in cupboards, in our day will not pass the test. What most of the people want when they ask for built-ins, are not cabinets that are built into the walls of the house, as the old-fashioned built-in cupboards were. They want counters and cabinets that are, in reality, built onto the walls of the room, rather than into the walls. Each of the three kitchens that were mentioned in chapter 9, had some form of an old built-in cup-

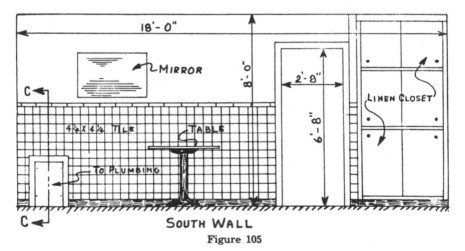

SOUTH WALL

Figure 105

board, that was either torn out completely, or else remodeled into a linen closet, as was the one shown in the last chapter. There are a number of reasons why this is true. First, plywood, masonite, sheetrock, and other processed materials are so much better for constructing up-to-date cabinets, than the materials that had to be used in the construction of the old-fashioned cupboards. The second reason is, that available power tools make it possible for a skilled mechanic with imagination and inventive ability, to turn almost any out-of-date kitchen into one that is, in many ways, as convenient as the latest thing in modern kitchens.

South Wall.—Fig. 105 gives the elevation of the south wall of the pattern kitchen shown in Fig. 87. To the right we have the linen closet that was treated in chapter 10. The 2'-8" x 6'-8" door opening shown, originally had a panel door that was almost always open. So the door was removed, which left a cased opening in its place. With modern heating systems many doors that

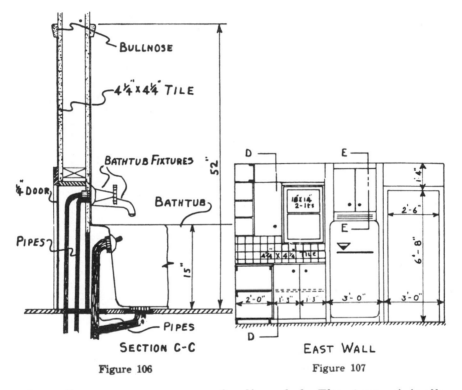

SECTION C-C

Figure 106

EAST WALL

Figure 107

formally were necessary, can be discarded. The stove originally was were the table is now shown. Directly under the mirror, as shown here, the old kitchen sink was located. The small door "to plumbing" gives access to the pipes of the bathtub. The size of this door must be determined by the existing circumstances. Section **C-C**, Fig. 106 shows the bathtub fixtures and the bathtub in part—also the pipe connections to the tub. The height of the wainscoting, both for the bathroom and the kitchen is given in figures. The bullnose and the 4¼" x 4¼" tile are pointed out on this drawing.

East Wall.—An elevation of the east wall is given by Fig. 107. This drawing gives some of the principal dimensions. Other important dimensions will be found with the details and

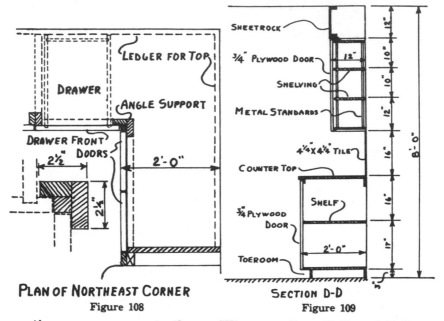

PLAN OF NORTHEAST CORNER
Figure 108

SECTION D-D
Figure 109

sections, as we come to them. Where sections **D-D** and **E-E** are cut, is shown on this elevation. A plan of the northeast corner

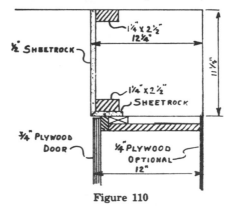

Figure 110

of the counter where it joins the east wall and also where it joints the north wall, is shown by Fig. 108. A larger scale drawing, showing the construction of the angle support, is shown inset, at the bottom left.

Section D-D.—A drawing of section **D-D,** is given by Fig. 109. This gives the names of the different parts of both the counter and the cabinet. Important dimensions are given here. A detail of the false work above the cabinet, showing the construction, is given by Fig. 110. How the cabinet joins the false work is also shown.

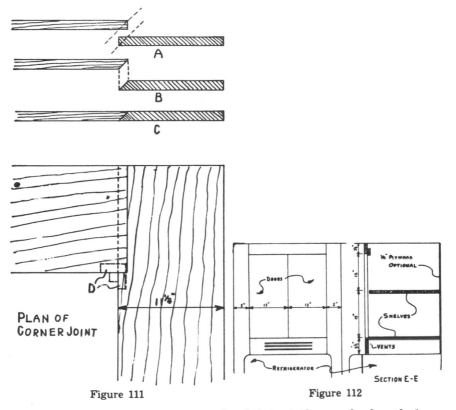

Figure 111   Figure 112

Shelving.—How to make the joint at the angle for shelves, is shown by Fig. 111. At **A, B, C** we have three edge views to the left, and three cross sections to the right, showing how to make the joint of the shelves at the angle. At **A,** by dotted lines, is shown how the two shelves are to be beveled; at **B** the bevels are shown cut, and the dotted lines show how the two pieces go together, and at **C** the joint is shown finished. At **D,**

by dotted lines, is shown how the boards have to be cut out to clear the angle support of the cabinet. The perpendicular dotted line that extends across the board, shows where the joint at the bottom comes together. This drawing shows a plan, in part, of the shelves at the angle of the cabinet.

Section E-E.—To the right of Fig. 112, section **E-E** is shown. To the left we have an elevation of the same cabinet, located directly over the refrigerator. The two drawings can be regarded as details of the cabinet.

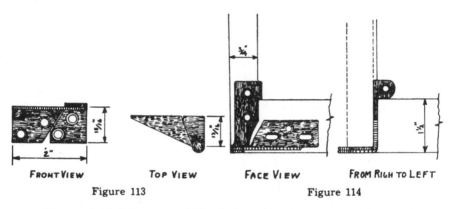

FRONT VIEW   TOP VIEW   FACE VIEW   FROM RIGH TO LEFT

Figure 113   Figure 114

Concealed Hinges.—All of the doors of the cabinets shown in this series of lessons, excepting those for the linen closet are fastened to the cabinets by means of concealed hinges. These hinges can be obtained at any up-to-date hardware store. There are two types of these hinges. One is shown by Fig. 113. To the left we have a front view of the hinge as it would appear fastened to the cabinet without the door fastened to it. To the right is shown a top view of the upper hinge (or a bottom view of a bottom hinge). These hinges are called concealed hinges, but the pivot part of the hinge is exposed to view when the hinge is in place and the door is closed. Fig. 114 shows the other type of concealed hinges—both types are made by the same concern. To the left we have a front view as the hinge is fastened to the cabinet, without the door. To the right is a view from right to left of the hinge in the position shown to the left. The dotted lines show the position of the door when in place.

Chapter 12

NORTH WALL AND DRAWERS

Light.—When the house was built with the kitchen that is taken here as a pattern, the owner wanted a kitchen with plenty of light. That part of it was ideal, but it did not go far enough. The kitchen otherwise was without the conveniences that are available today—conveniences that are necessary in any kitchen, if it is to pass as modern. If the reader will refer to Figs. 86 and 87, he will see what the kitchen was like before and what it is after it was remodeled. When this remodeling was under consideration, the householder thought that perhaps the triple window should be cut down to a twin window. But when this was submitted to the housewife, she objected—she wanted the

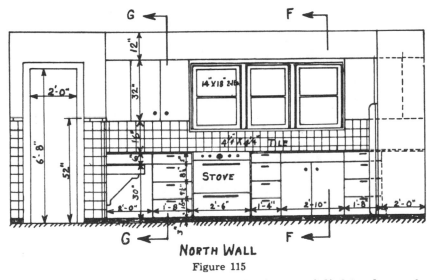

NORTH WALL

Figure 115

triple window, because she wanted plenty of light where she prepared food for her household, and that settled it.

North Wall.—Fig. 115 is an elevation of the north wall of our pattern kitchen. Here at the extreme left we have the door to the pantry. To the right of the pantry is the housewife's desk—next to it, drawers—the range—more drawers—then the cabinet under the sink, and another set of drawers. A profile of the cabinet that encloses the refrigerator and extends up to the ceiling is shown to the extreme right. All of this can be seen in plan by turning to the drawings Figs. 86 and 87 of our pattern kitchen.

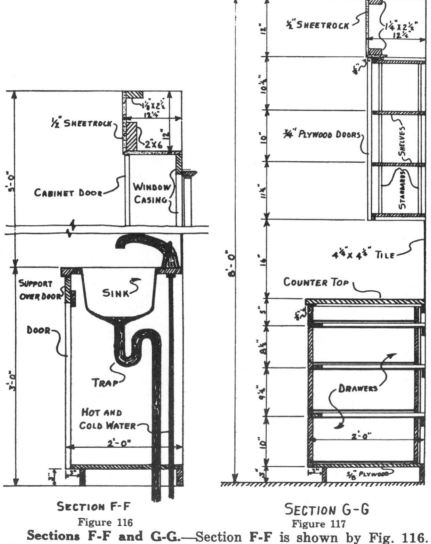

Section F-F

Figure 116

Section G-G

Figure 117

Sections F-F and G-G.—Section F-F is shown by Fig. 116. Here we have, let's start at the top, the construction of the

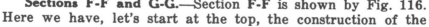

dropped ceiling directly over the triple window. The back edge of the sheetrock is fastened to the upper edge of the head window casings, while the front part is carried by a 2″ x 6″, which in addition to carrying the load, answers as nailer for the sheetrock. It should be pointed out here, that the sheetrock is mitered at the angle. This makes an excellent corner finish —in case there should be some open places, due to chipping of

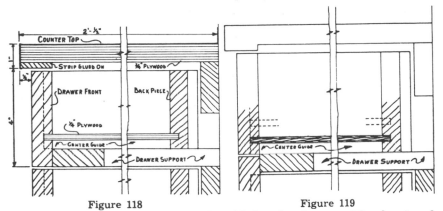

Figure 118   Figure 119

the sheetrock, such places should be fixed up with sheetrock finisher, just as the other sheetrock joints are fixed. Fig. 116, bottom part of this drawing, gives a cross section of the sink and the cabinet that supports it. Fig. 117 is a drawing of section **G-G.** The false work shown here should be noticed. In this

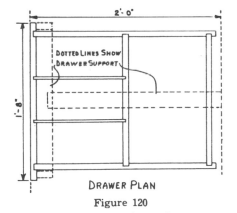

DRAWER PLAN

Figure 120

case, the cabinet was set first. Then the narrow strip of sheet-rock was put in place, in such a manner, that it would project

¼-inch beyond the doors of the cabinet, as shown on the drawing. With the cabinets constructed as shown, the bottom piece
of sheetrock of the false work, does not need to extend back to
the wall, excepting over the triple window. This should be
studied. The bottom part of the drawing gives a cross section
of the set of drawers, which should be compared with Figs. 118
and 119, details of the construction of the top drawer. The
construction of the other drawers is the same. The front and
the back are shown in these details. The drawers have plywood
bottoms, and are supported by T-shaped drawer supports. Onto
these drawer supports the center guide is fastened. Fig. 119

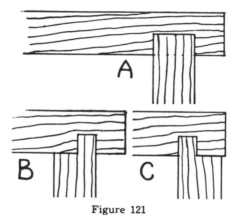

Figure 121

shows how the depth of the drawer can be increased by lower-
ing the bottom. The dotted lines give the position of the drawer
bottom as it is shown by Fig. 118, while the shaded drawer bottom is in the position that increases the depth of the drawer.
It will be noticed in this drawing that the drawer front of the
next drawer below, extends up and laps onto the front part
of the drawer support.

Drawer Construction.—A plan of the small drawer, shown
in detail by Figs. 118 and 119, is shown in plan by Fig. 120.
The T-shaped drawer support is indicated here by dotted lines.
Also shown here are three small compartments in the front
half of the drawer, and one large compartment in the back half
— the construction of the joints should be noted. Fig. 121
shows details of three different ways to make simple joints for
drawers. At **A** is shown the joint used in the drawers shown.
At **B** is shown a joint that might be an improvement over the

one shown at **A.** At **C** we have a joint that is in reverse of the one shown at **B.** The only justification for using the joint shown at **C,** is using it to increase the length of the inside dimension

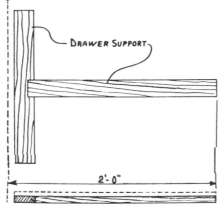

Figure 122

of the drawer. In this case the length would be increased by a little less than ½-inch. One-half of an inch in a short drawer could, under certain conditions, increase its usefulness.

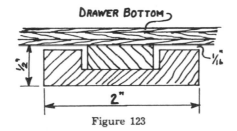

Figure 123

Drawer Support and Center Guide. — Fig. 122 shows two drawings of the T-shaped drawer support. The upper drawing shows the support in plan, while the bottom drawing gives a side view. The dotted line in the bottom drawing indicates the position of the center guide when it is in place. Fig. **123** is a drawing of an approved center guide. The grooved part of this guide is fastened to the drawer support with glue and small brads, while the other part is fastened in the same way, to the bottom of the drawer. A comparison of this center guide with the center guides shown by Fig. 90, should be made. All of these guides, if properly installed give satisfactory service.

Chapter 13

PANTRY AND BATHROOM

Pantries.—There are still a great many pantries in daily use, and there are still many housewives, who would not do without their pantry. Pantries are not coming back in the sense that every new home will have one, but the housewife who has a conveniently located and well arranged pantry, will continue to use it, and it is quite likely, that if she ever has a part in making plans for a new home, she will insist on a pantry, or something that will answer as a substitute for a pantry.

A plan of the pantry that went with the pattern kitchen, which was discussed in the previous chapter, is shown by Fig.

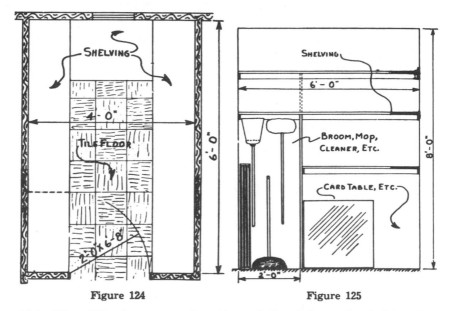

Figure 124   Figure 125

124. Fig. 125 shows an elevation of the left wall of this plan. Here we have three shelves that are intended to hold rather large utensils or other large objects that are necessities in a home, especially in the kitchen. To the left is shown a place for brooms, mops, cleaners and so forth. This is located to the left

of the pantry entrance. To the right of the drawing there is floor and wall space for storing card tables and the like. Fig. 126 gives a cross section of the pantry, showing the window in

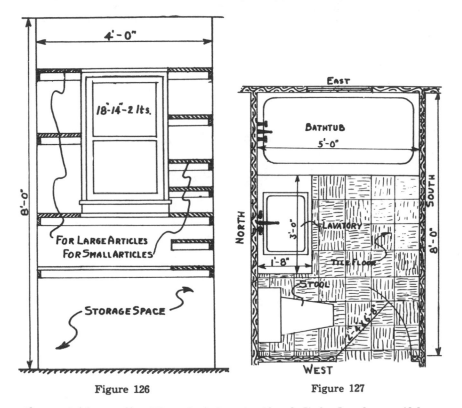

Figure 126   Figure 127

the outside wall. The shelving to the left is for large things, as already mentioned, but to the right the shelving arrangement will accommodate small and medium articles. There is also storage space below the window and under the shelving of the wall to the right.

Modernizing Homes.—This is a field, (as mentioned in a previous chapter, in which the progressive carpenter can carry on and build up a business of his own. This suggestion should be remembered by the student as he reads and studies these discussions. Almost any well-built house, no matter how old-fashioned it might be, can be modernized. What such householders want is somebody who can first, work out the details, and then do the work in a manner that will be a credit to himself, and satisfactory to the householder.

Bathroom.—Fig. 127 gives the floor plan of the modernized bathroom that belonged to the old-fashioned home taken here as an overall pattern for these discussions. The changes were:

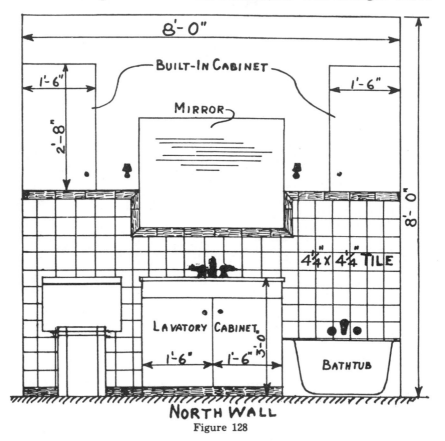

NORTH WALL

Figure 128

Bathtub with fixtures, cabinet lavatory, stool, and tile floor. Fig. 128 shows additional changes that were made on the north wall, namely, two built-in cabinets for towels and other bathroom necessities, a mirror with a light to the right and left, and the tile wainscoting. Fig. 129 shows a cross section and the east wall. Here, by dotted lines, is shown how the cabinets are built into the wall, with part of them extending into the room. The cabinet shown to the left is built into the north wall, while the medicine cabinet shown to the right is built into the south wall. A cross section is given on this figure, of the lavatory and the cabinet that supports it.

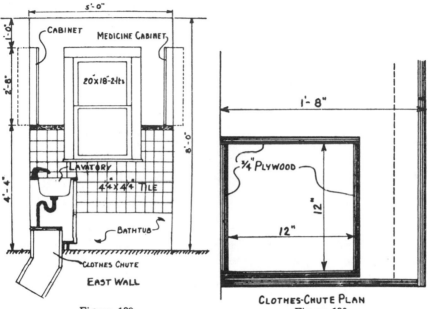

Figure 129   CLOTHES-CHUTE PLAN
                          Figure 130

Clothes Chute.—The clothes chute shown toward the bottom of Fig. 129 is given in details in Figs. 130 and 131. Fig. 130 shows the floor plan of that part of the lavatory cabinet, where the clothes chute is located. The drawing specifies ¾-inch plywood, but the chute can be made of ordinary lumber with good results. Fig. 131 shows how to build the chute so it will drop the clothes where it should, rather than directly under it. The part marked **A** was cut away as shown at **B,** from the part marked **C.**

Medicine Cabinet.—Fig. 132 shows the elevation of the south wall. Here are shown the wainscoting, the medicine cabinet and the different dimensions of this figure. Fig. 133 to the right, shows a face view of the medicine cabinet without the doors in place. The doors are to be slab doors, such as have been shown for the kitchen in the previous illustrations. They are hung with concealed hinges. The shelving here, is made of ⅜-inch material, while the frame is made of ¾-inch boards. To the left is shown a cross section of the right half of the medicine

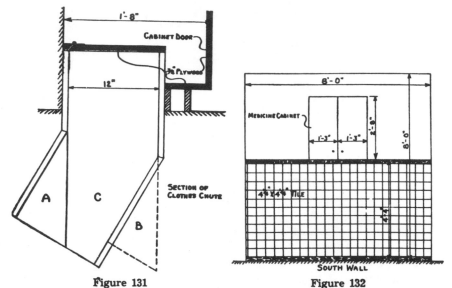

Figure 131   Figure 132

cabinet. Notice the small shelves, which make possible additional storage space for small objects, such as small bottles, boxes, and so forth. The doors are indicated by the dotted line to the left.

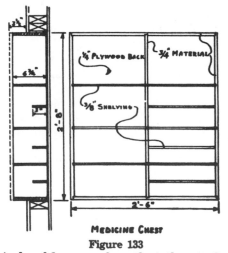

MEDICINE CHEST

Figure 133

The student should remember that the explanations and the drawings of these chapters, are hypothetical, and therefore open for modifications—they should not be taken as hard and fast.

Chapter 14

MODERNIZED KITCHENS

A Fertile Field.—In previous discussion of built-in cabinets, reference was made to old kitchens in this writer's neighborhood, that were modernized recently. One of those kitchens will be used as a pattern for a series of four chapters dealing with modernizing old kitchens. It should again be pointed out, that this is a wide and fertile field for the carpenter who is prepared for it, for there are a great many old kitchens in every vicinity that should be made modern. First, the carpenter who would make this his special field, must be able to give the pro-

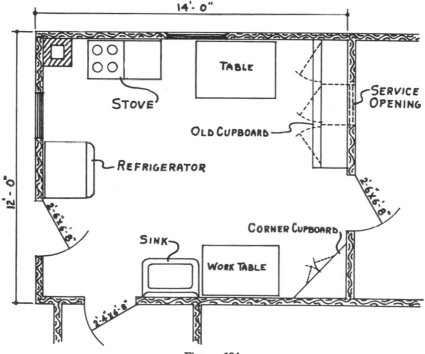

Figure 134

spective customers original ideas in remodeling kitchens; and second, he must be in a position to do the work economically and well. Poor workmanship and excessive costs are among the worst advertising means, that any businessman can employ However, this does not mean, that cheap work is desirable as a means of succeeding in business. "Cheap" and "economical" are not synonymous in the sense that they are used here. The businessman who wants to succeed must furnish something that will fill the needs of his customers, at a cost that the customers can afford.

Old Kitchen.—Fig. 134 shows the old kitchen that is used as an example of kitchens that should be modernized. The drawing

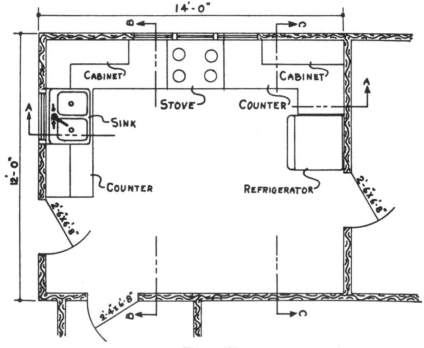

Figure 135

gives the arrangement of the furniture and the old cupboards, one a corner cupboard and the other one with an opening through the wall from the kitchen to the dining room. After studying this arrangement, see Fig. 135, which shows the arrangement after the remodeling was completed. A triple window replaces a single window that previously provided light for the range and table. The present arrangement gives ample light for the range, and for the counter on either side of the range. The sink is placed in front of a single window, shown to the left of the drawing. This setup leaves the area for traffic and portable kitchen furniture, unobstructed.

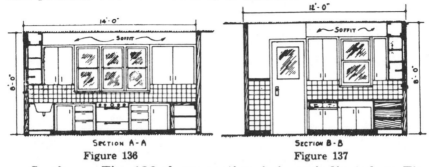

Section A-A
Figure 136

Section B-B
Figure 137

Sections.—Fig. 136 shows section **A-A,** as indicated on Fig. 135, showing the face view of the counter, the triple window, and the hung cabinets. Here we have the range at the center, with a set of drawers on either side. There is a door to the right and another to the left, opening to counter cabinets. To the extreme right and left are shown cross sections of the counter. Above we have from left to right, a cross section of a cabinet, the front of another cabinet, the triple window, and still another

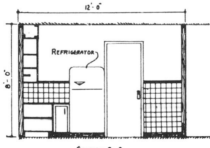

Section C-C
Figure 138

cabinet. Just below the ceiling, to the left, is shown a cross section of the soffit. A face view of the soffit is shown above the triple window and the two cabinets. Fig. 137 shows section **B-B,** as indicated on Fig. 135. Here, from left to right, we have the outside door; a counter cabinet with two drawers, and a hung cabinet above; the cabinet under the sink and the window above; a one-door cabinet and, to the extreme right, a cross section of the cabinet and the soffit above; also a cross section of a set of the drawers in the counter. Section **C-C,** Fig. 138, to the left, shows a cross section of the counter and a hung cabinet above. The refrigerator and the door to the dining room are shown toward the center.

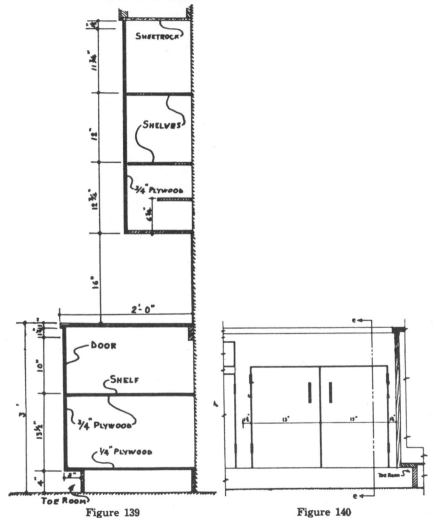

Figure 139   Figure 140

Details of Cabinets.—Fig. 139 shows a cross section, in a larger scale, of the counter and hung cabinet above it. From the bottom up, we have, a 4-inch base, allowing 3″ x 4″ for toe room; a ¼-inch plywood cabinet bottom; ¾-inch plywood shelf and door, and a plywood counter top, covered with a suitable counter-top finish. (There are a number of counter-top finishing materials on the market, that give excellent service, which should be selected by the owner, so as to conform with his tastes and means. The bottom of the hung cabinet is 16 inches above the counter top. The shelves should be noted, which are gained into the sides of the cabinet. The little shelf at the bottom is very practical for holding small-can canned goods. It should be pointed out that the sheetrock, used on the soffit, forms the top of the hung cabinet.

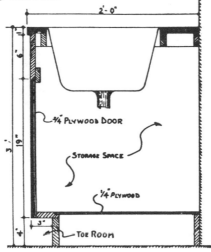

SECTION e-e
Figure 141

The front of the counter cabinet under the sink is shown by Fig. 140. The surface of the doors is kept flush with the surface of the frame. This can be seen to the right, where a cross section of a door to another cabinet is shown. At the bottom is shown a cross section of the toe room. A section cut through **e-e,** is shown by Figure 141. This detail also shows the door flush with the frame. The figures here give the information necessary to construct this cabinet. The space under the sink, as indicated on the drawing, is used for storage purposes.

This chapter on built-in cabinets, deals largely with basic things. As we go along more and more details will be presented, until at the end, those who read carefully, both the lines and between the lines, will be able to construct built-ins that will give satisfactory service.

Chapter 15

BUILT-IN CABINETS

Old-Fashioned Houses.—Many of the younger readers might wonder why kitchens and, for that matter, houses were built a few generations ago, as they were. The answer is simple: In those days they built, just as we are doing today, the best that they could, with the materials available, and the means with which such materials could be secured. Basic natural building materials were plentiful and, as a rule, were available at reasonable costs. The same was true of labor. Most of the processed building materials that we have, were unknown to them, while processed materials that they knew and used, with few exceptions, are obsolete or unknown to us. It is this writers opinion, that in the next few generations the changes in

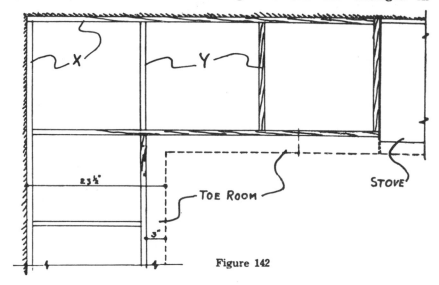

Figure 142

processed building materials, will be much greater and more revolutionary, than they were in the last few generations. The builders then, will wonder about the builders of today.

Built-In Cabinet Base.—Fig. 142 is a plan, showing in part, the things that are done first, in erecting built-in kitchen cabi-

76

nets. What is shown here is the rough part of the base. Properly sized ⅞-inch material is set on edge, which receives the first floor and supports the cabinet and what is in it. Sometimes the piece that is nailed against the wall, marked **X**, is omitted, without damaging results. In the same way, the cross pieces, marked **Y**, can be omitted, using only the front and back supports for the floor.

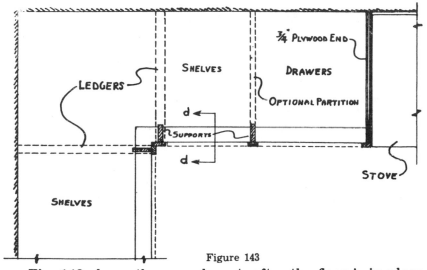

Figure 143

Fig. 143 shows the same layout, after the floor is in place. Here the dotted lines should be noted. Cross sections of the frames for the front of the cabinets are shown shaded, and the

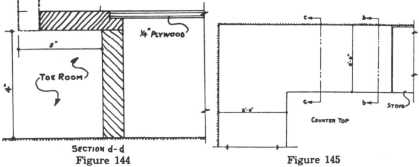

SECTION d-d
Figure 144

Figure 145

doors for the cabinets are indicated by dotted lines. The supports to which the frames are fastened are pointed out. These support the front of the counter top. The ledgers, shown by dotted lines, reinforce the counter between the front support and the wall, leaving the space open under the counter, so that the corner area can be utilized. Sometimes, one or both of these counter supports are made of solid partitions, similar to the optional partition indicated by dotted lines. When both of

Figure 146

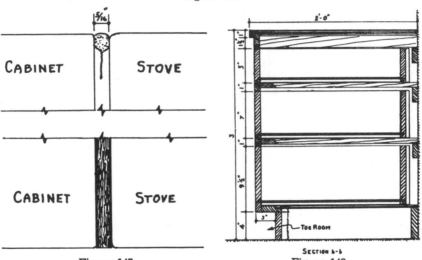

Figure 147　　　　　　Figure 148

these parts of the counter are supported by partitions it renders the corner area useless. The end of the counter next to the stove, is made of ¾-inch plywood, and supports that part of the counter top. Section **d-d** is shown in detail by Fig. 144, giving the construction of the base around the toe room. It also shows how the ¼-inch plywood floor is joined to the ⅞-inch piece over the toe room.

Counter Top.—Fig. 145 shows the counter top of the part we are using here as a pattern for constructing these cabinets. The width, as shown, is 2 feet. This width makes the material work out with a minimum of waste. The allowance between the counter top and the range should be from ¼- to 5/16-inch. This size opening is just right for using a piece of weather stripping for closing the crack between the range and the counter top, after the range is in position. Fig. 146 shows to the left a cross section of the weather stripping, and to the right we have a side view. How the weather stripping goes into the crack is shown

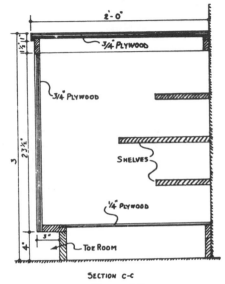

SECTION C-C

Figure 149

by Fig. 147. The upper drawing gives a cross section and the bottom one is a plan, in part. This particluar kind of weather stripping is available at almost all hardware stores.

Sections b-b and c-c.—Fig. 148 is a cross section through **b-b** in Fig. 145. The 3" x 4" toe room is shown at the bottom, left. The other figures from top down are 1 inch for the counter top nosing, 1½ inches for the head piece of the frame, 5 inches for the top drawer, 1 inch for the top cross bar, 7 inches for the second drawer, 1 inch for the second cross bar, 9½ inches for the bottom drawer, and 4 nches for toe room. Fig. 149 is a cross section through **c-c**, as shown by Fig. 145. This gives the figures of the important parts of the cabinet. The two quarter-width and one-half width shelves, makes this part of the cabinet an excellent storage place for small-can canned goods. Then there is space on and below the front half of the half-width shelf for containers, such as bottles, etc., that can not be stored on the smaller spaces. In front of the shelves there is space for things that need a great deal of head-room, as it were.

Chapter 16

DETAILS OF DRAWERS

Skill.—Does the present-day mechanic have as much skill as the mechanic of fifty years ago? Let's see, skill is to know how to do, and able to do, a particular line of work perfectly. It is more than what is often referred to as "the know-how." It is, as this writer sees it, the "know-how-and-do-well" — in short, it is the thing that makes a finished mechanic, out of an untrained apprentice. This ability can not be acquired from books alone—books do furnish much of the technical knowledge,

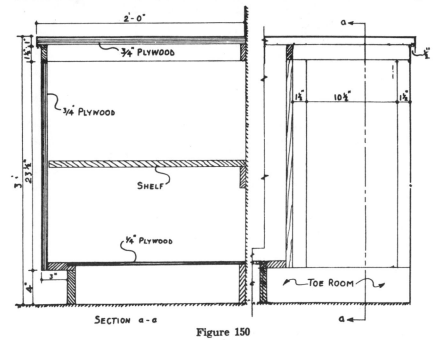

Figure 150

but that isn't all of it. The indispensable part of skill is gained by the process of "learning to do by doing." This brings up a second question: Does the present-day mechanic have as much opportunity to learn to do by doing, as the old timers had? The average old-timer of fifty years ago was far ahead of the present-day mechanic, in hand work, because almost everything he did was hand work. Few, very few of the old-timers that this writer knew during his apprenticeship, knew very much, if anything, about handling power tools. In fact, power tools as they are known today, were nonexistent. The conclusion; therefore, is that the mechanic of fifty years ago was more skillful in hand work, than the mechanic of today. But, on the other hand, the present-day mechanic is far ahead, when it come to working with power tools.

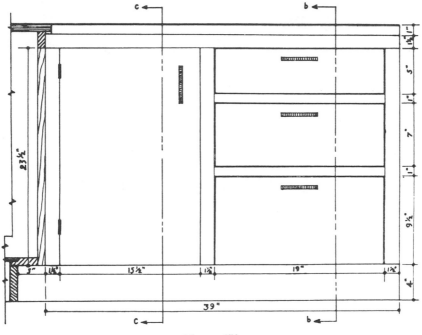

Figure 151

Cabinets and Drawers.—Fig. 150 shows to the right, a face view of a one-door cabinet. To the left is shown a cross section of this cabinet, cut through **a-a**. The figures and notes on the drawings give enough information to guide the workman in constructing such a cabinet. The floor plan and cross sections of our pattern kitchen, are shown in chapter 14. A section of this plan, cut through **A-A, Fig. 135** is shown by **Fig. 136.**

Fig. 151 shows a one-door cabinet and a set of three drawers located to the left of the range, and Fig. 152 shows a similar layout, but in reverse order, on the right of the range, as shown in chapter 14, Figs. 135 and 136.

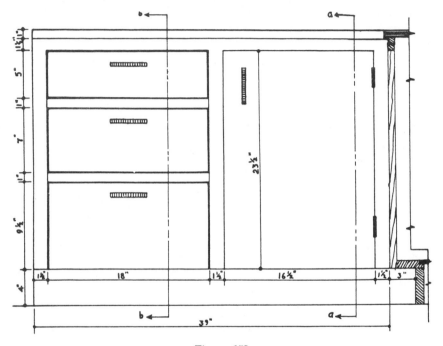

Figure 152

Details of Drawers.—Fig. 153 shows at the top a cross section of the drawer shown in plan just below it. The ¼-inch plywood drawer bottom is pointed out. To the right we have the other cross section of the same drawer. This shows the two sides, the plywood bottom, and the center guide. The joints of this drawer should be noticed, especially those that join the drawer front to the sides. A larger scale detail of the front joints is shown by Fig. 154. This is a secure joint and not hard to make, however, it should be put together with a good quality glue.

Details of Center Guide.—An edge view of the center guide is shown by the top drawing of Fig. 155. To the right is shown a good wall support for the back of this guide. The bottom drawing shows a plan of the same guide, also showing the back wall support. A little study of these two views will give the student a good idea of its construction. The dotted lines, at the top and bottom, left, show how the front guide support is

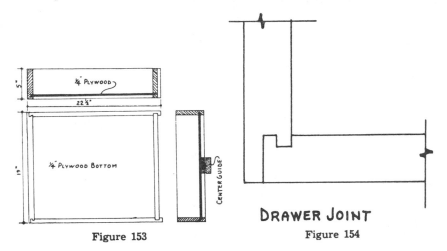

Figure 153

DRAWER JOINT

Figure 154

fastened to the upright counter supports, one on either side of the drawers. To the right a cross section of the center guide is again given. The space between the drawer bottom and the

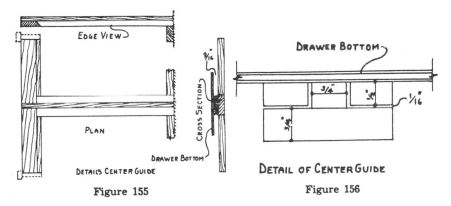

DETAILS CENTER GUIDE

Figure 155

DETAIL OF CENTER GUIDE

Figure 156

frame of the center guide is given here as 9/16-inch. Fig. 156 shows a detail in a larger scale of the center guide, giving important dimensions. The parts without figures are not important and can be determined by the workman.

Cabinet with Drawers.—Fig. 157 is a face view of a cabinet with two small drawers at the top. The bottom part has two doors. From top down, we have, 1 inch for counter nosing, 1½ inch for head, 4½ inches for drawer, 1½ inches for cross bar, 17½ inches for door, and 4 inches for toe room. A cross section through **f-f,** is shown by Fig. 158.

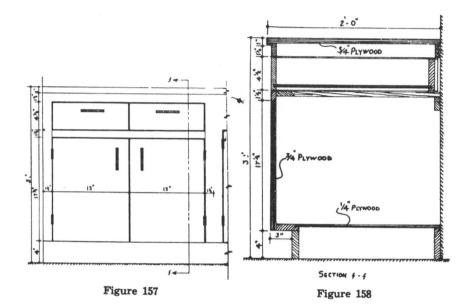

Figure 157   Figure 158

This chapter, as well as the chapter that is to follow, should be studied in keeping with the two chapters that have gone before. References to the illustrations should be made whether or not they have been referred to in the text.

Chapter 17

JOINTS, SECTIONS AND SOFFIT

Hand and Power Tools.—When this writer was serving his apprenticeship (it was not called an apprenticeship, but that is what it was) he worked on built-in cabinets for a rather large pantry. The owners were wealthy, and for that reason wanted the best that was in vogue at the time. The ceiling was high, and the cabinets extended up to the ceiling. The upper part of the cabinets had two sets of doors. One set covered the shelves that were reachable without a stepladder, and the other set of shorter doors went up to the head casing, which was fitted to the ceiling. They were panel doors, and hand made. The frame, which was grooved for the panel, was put together with mortice-and-tenon joints. All of this work was done with hand tools. There was not a single power

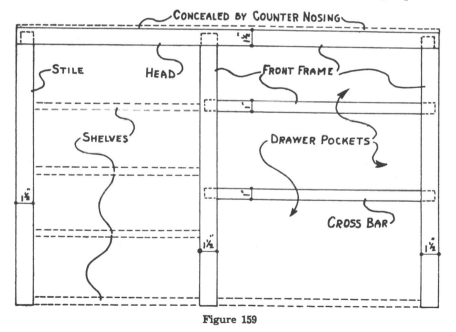

Figure 159

tool on the job, and probably not available at the time. A plow and a miter box were necessities in those days.

Today it is different: We have portable power tools, such as table saws, skill saws, power drills, sanders, and other power-driven tools, that simplify the field carpenter's work. Properly equipped with power tools, he can do cabinet work that cannot be excelled anywhere.

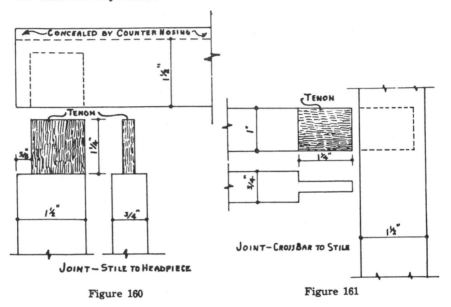

Figure 160   Figure 161

Front Frames.—Fig. 159 shows the front frame for the cabinet and set of drawers, shown immediately to the left of the range, as shown in Figs. 135 and 136 of chapter 14. To the right of the range is shown a duplicate, in reverse, of what is shown to the left. Face views, in a larger scale, of those two fronts, are shown in chapter 16, Figs. 151 and 152. What we have in Fig. 159, shows the frame, or better stated, the casings, nailed to the body of the cabinet. The mortice-and-tenon joints used to join the different pieces, are shown by dotted lines. The shelves are indicated by horizontal dotted lines. Study this drawing in keeping with the drawings referred to.

Mortice-and-Tenon Joints.—Fig. 160 gives details of a mortice-and-tenon joint. The head mortice is indicated by dotted lines. Two views of the tenon, shaded, are shown by the bottom drawings. The dimensions are given by figures. Details of the mortice-and-tenon joints, where the cross bars join the stiles, are given by Fig. 161.

Hung Cabinets.—The face view of a hung cabinet, before the casings have been nailed on, is shown by Fig. 162. (See Fig. 139, chapter 14. The optional piece shown at the top is indicated by the horizontal dotted line. When this piece is omitted, the soffit closes the top of the case. The shelves are shown gained into the sides of the cabinet. Fig. 163 shows the same layout, after the

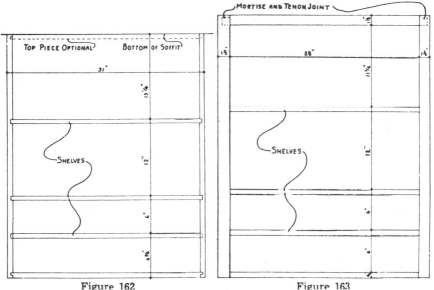

Figure 162   Figure 163

casings have been nailed in place. Fig. 164 shows the completed front of the cabinet, with the doors hinged to the frame and the handles attached. It should be pointed out that the doors in all of the cabinets covered are fitted, so as to bring the surface of the doors flush with the surface of the casings.

Cross Sections of Cabinets.—Fig. 165, left, gives a cross section of a hung cabinet that has a back of ¼-inch plywood. This back is nailed to the back of the case and the shelves. The top and bottom pieces and the sides are rabetted to receive the back, as shown by the drawing at the top and at the bottom. To the right we have a cabinet that has no back or top piece. The strips of board, marked **1, 2, 3,** and **4,** run from one side of the case to the other, and are nailed to the back of the shelves and to the sides of the cabinet. When the cabinet is hung to the wall, these strips are nailed to the studding. If the soffit is installed first, then a nailer, number **5,** must be fastened to the wall to receive the sheetrock. But if the cabinet is hung first, then the sheetrock is nailed to strip numbered **1** and the head casing to the left.

Soffit Construction.—Two details of soffit construction are shown by Fig. 166. To the left we show a soffit, that was constructed after the cabinets were hung to the wall. The procedure is this:

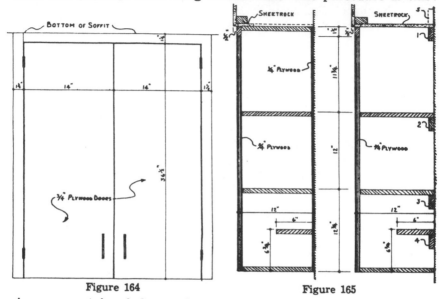

Figure 164   Figure 165

A narrow strip of sheetrock is fastened to the top of the cabinets, as shown at the bottom, left. Then a 1⅛″x3″ nailer is nailed on top of the sheetrock strip, as shown. Another nailer is nailed to the ceiling, shown to the top, left. This done, the front piece

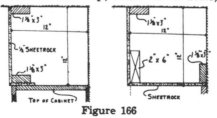

Figure 166

of sheetrock is put in place. If the sheetrock is carefully cut to a miter, by hand with a saw, a good sharp corner can be obtained. The other method is to cut the sheetrock square across, and use a corner bead to give it a sharp corner. The detail to the right, shows the construction of the soffit from cabinet to cabinet, above the windows. The 2″x6″ is used to bridge the distance between cabinets, and at the same time answer for nailer.

Chapter 18

SMALL APARTMENT

Apartments.—In this era of industry, when whole families leave the farm and go to live in urban areas, apartments are much in demand. This applies to apartments ranging from family size down to apartments accommodating only one person. The trend from rural areas to urban areas is opening up a field of remodeling for carpenters. Old and out-of-date houses are remodeled so as to accommodate two, three, or even more tenants. Consequently opportunities for carpenters, who have the imagination, ability, and stamina, will be met on every hand. Here is a field for the men who can qualify, to establish themselves in a profitable business in their own right.

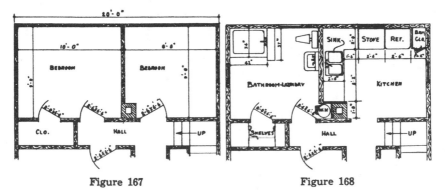

Figure 167   Figure 168

Old Layout.—Fig. 167 gives a drawing of two bedrooms, closet, hall, and a stairway in part. This area of the second floor of an old house was changed into a bathroom-laundry, and kitchen for the second-floor apartment.

New Layout.—Fig. 168 gives the plan after the remodeling. The purpose here is not to show an ideal plan for a bathroom, laundry, linen closet, and kitchen; but it is to suggest how, with but little changing, a very satisfactory arrangement can be obtained, which could be called ideal under the existing circumstances.

Kitchen.—The kitchen is shown to the upper right in Fig. 168. Here we have the sink, the range, the refrigerator, and the broom closet. An elevation of the left wall of the kitchen is shown by

Fig. 169. Fig. 170, to the left, shows a cross section of the cabinets, section **A-A.** To the right we have the elevation of this part of the cabinets. Section **B-B** is shown to the left of Fig. 171, while

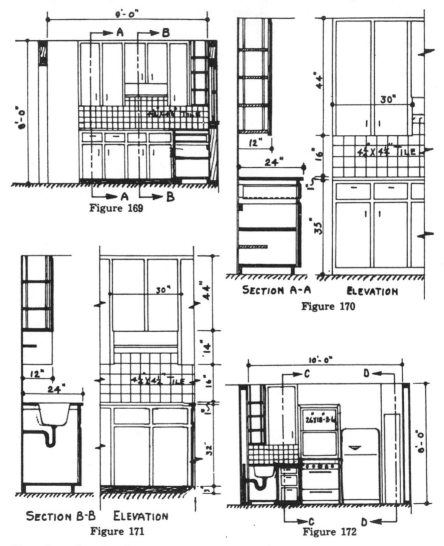

Figure 169

SECTION A-A   ELEVATION

Figure 170

SECTION B-B   ELEVATION

Figure 171

Figure 172

the elevation is shown to the right. The wall space between the counter and the upper cabinet is covered with 4¼-inch by 4¼-inch tile. The counter on both sides of the sink should be covered with a suitable counter topping. This material should be selected by the owner, after he has examined the different kinds of counter toppings on the market.

Fig. 172 shows an elevation of the part shown at the top in Fig. 168, representing the kitchen. Here we have a cross section of the cabinets, face views of the drawers, range, refrigerator,

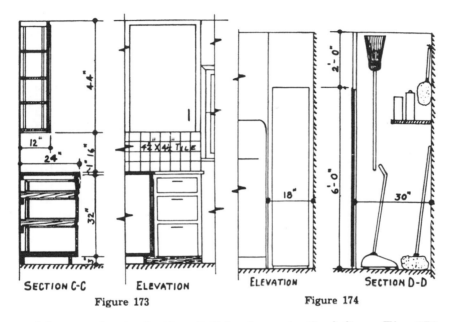

SECTION C-C   ELEVATION   ELEVATION   SECTION D-D

Figure 173   Figure 174

and broom closet. Section **C-C** is shown to the left on Fig. 173, and the elevation of this part is shown to the right. Fig. 174 shows section **D-D** to the right, and a face view of it to the left.

Cross Sections.—Cross sections in a larger scale, of the top and bottom cabinets as shown by section **C-C**, Fig. 173, are shown by Figs. 175 and 176. Here are given figures and other information that is necessary for constructing the cabinets. On Fig. 175 are pointed out from top to bottom, the tile between the top and bottom cabinets, the counter top, and the center guides. The drawers are shown shaded, details of which will be given in the next chapter. To the left, Fig. 176, is shown the upper cabinet. Pointed out are the metal standards and shelves. To the right is a detail showing how the lipped doors contact the casings of the cabinet.

Material.—For the upper cabinet use 1-inch by 12-inch material, both for the sides and for the shelves. Use ¾-inch plywood for the doors. For the bottom cabinet use ¾-inch material for the counter top and the wide shelves. Use ¾-inch material for the drawers and the other parts of the cabinet.

Hardware.—There are different kinds of hinges for lipped cabinet doors on the market. Some of them are almost concealed,

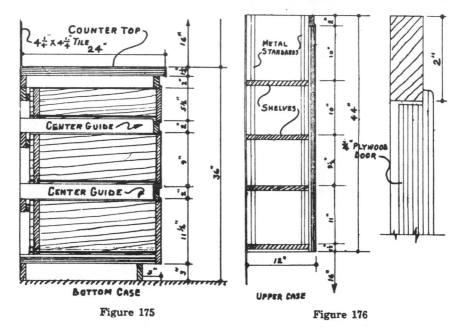

Figure 175　　　　　　　　　　Figure 176

while others are fastened to the face of the door. The exposed parts of these hinges are of an ornamental design, which adds much to the appearance of the cabinet doors. There are also a number of different kinds of cabinet door catches on the market. For pulls, either knobs or handles can be used. This applies both to the doors and the drawers. There is a big variety of cabinet door pulls and handles on the market, that should satisfy almost anybody's tastes. This is also true of catches.

Chapter 19

DRAWERS AND PIPE CABINET

Plywood.—The availability of plywood and other materials that are used today in building cabinets, have made possible the modern built-in cabinets. This feature of the modern home is a very important consideration for the home builder. But for the person who wants to buy or rent a house, it is a decisive first consideration. For those families who can afford it, will not be without well-planned built-in cabinets. For this reason the built-in feature of the modern home is here to stay, and to be improved whenever and wherever it can be improved.

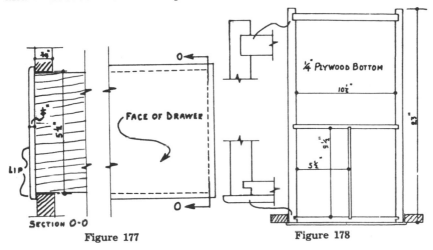

Figure 177   Figure 178

Drawer Lips.—Fig. 177, to the right, shows a part of the top drawer front, shown in Fig. 175 of the previous chapter. (Everything that will be said in this chapter, will have reference to the drawers shown in Fig. 175 of the previous chapter. The dotted lines to the right, top and bottom of this view, indicate the offset for the lips. Section **O-O** is shown to the left, where are given various dimensions in figures. The lips of the other drawers are the same as shown here.

Plan and Joints of Drawers.—Fig 178 shows a plan of the top drawer referred to, with two partitions in it. At the upper left, is a detail of the joints for the back, while to the bottom left, is shown a good joint for the front. The plans of the other drawers are the same as this one, excepting the partitions.

Longway Section of Drawers.—Fig. 179 shows a longway section of the center drawer, showing its relationship to the center guides of the drawer above and the center guide on which it rests. Pointed

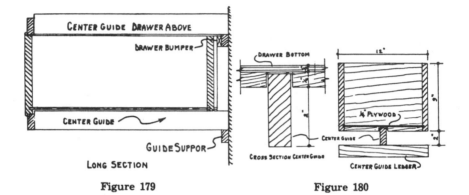

Figure 179   Figure 180

out are the drawer bumper, center guide, and guide support. Fig. 180, to the right, shows a cross section of the drawer, center guide, and guide ledger or support. To the left is a detail of the center

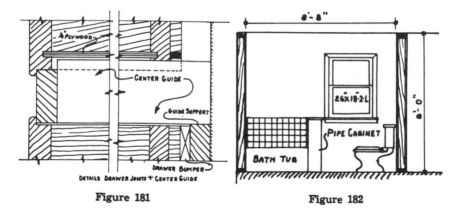

Figure 181   Figure 182

guide, showing its relationship to the drawer it supports. Fig. 181 shows details in part, of the center guide, drawer above and drawer below. Pointed out are, the plywood drawer bottom, center guide,

guide support, and drawer bumper. The drawer bumpers are very important, for without them the lips of the drawers would eventually crack or break off.

Pipe Cabinet of Bathtub.—The elevation shown by Fig. 182, shows the upper wall of the bathroom-laundry, shown in Fig. 168 of the previous chapter. In this elevation are shown the corner bathtub, pipe cabinet, window, and stool. Fig. 183, to the left

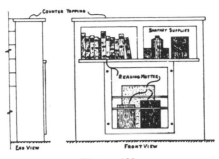

Figure 183

shows an end view of the pipe cabinet, and to the right is shown the front of the cabinet, with a book shelf, a shelf for sanitary supplies, and a rack for reading matter—magazines and so forth. To the left, Fig. 184 is shown a cross section of the cabinet, while

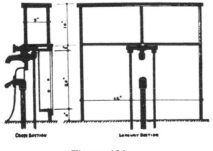

Figure 184

to the right we have a longway section. The pipes that lead to the bathtub are shown heavily shaded. The first purpose of the cabinet is to conceal the pipes, while the second purpose is the provision for sanitary supplies and reading matter.

Originality.—The book case and reading matter rack was original with the owner. The carpenter was thinking of fastening a piece of plywood over the opening that provided access to the pipes, when the owner, standing by, suggested making a rack for reading matter. The idea was original and was carried out. The rack was made and fastened to the cabinet with screws, as shown; thus, when the plumber wants to get to the pipes, he merely removes the rack and goes to work.

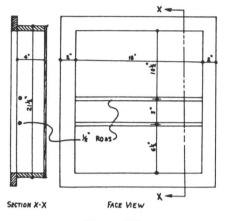

Figure 185

Magazine Rack.—Fig. 185, to the right, shows a face view of the reading matter rack, and to the left is shown section **X-X.** The rods pointed out, can either be wood or metal. This rack is fastened on with screws, so that it can be removed when something goes wrong with the pipes.

Chapter 20

LAZY SUSAN FEATURES

In reality these features could be called accessories to cabinets and built-ins. In their right place they are practical conveniences, and at the same time novelties. They can be put to a great many different uses, not only in the field of cabinets and built-ins, but in other fields as well. Space will not permit a thorough coverage, even if limited to the field of cabinets and built-ins. The interested student, if what we show in this chapter does not meet his needs, should check on what he can find on

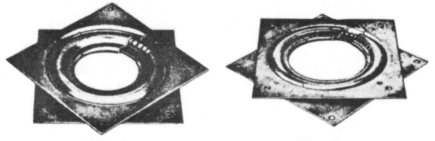

3″ Bearing   4″ Bearing

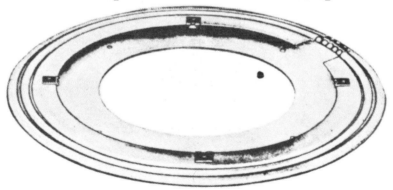

12″ Bearing

Figure 186

the market, where as time goes on, new and perhaps improved designs will be available. Modifications are always possible and in order.

Lazy Susan.—The upper drawing, Fig. 186 shows the 3-inch size of turntable ball bearing. At the right a 4-inch size is shown, and at the bottom we have the 12-inch size. The 6-inch size is not shown, but in principle it is the same as those shown. Fig. 187, upper drawing, shows a cross section of the smaller bearings, indicating how the device is fastened to the surface on

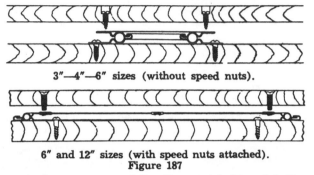

3″—4″—6″ sizes (without speed nuts).

6″ and 12″ sizes (with speed nuts attached).
Figure 187

which it rests by screws, while the revolving object, whatever it might be, is fastened to the upper surface of the device. This might be a circular or even square shelf that revolves on the bearing or swivel. It also might be a sort of tray or a series of shelves, depending on the needs of the situation and the desires of the owners.

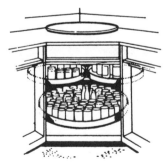

Lazy Susan

Corner Cupboard Shelves
Figure 188

The bottom drawing gives a cross section of the 12-inch bearing, also which is fastened to the surface on which it rests, while the upper surface, with the speed nuts, receives the thing that is to revolve.

Different Uses.—Fig. 188 shows a corner cabinet with three revolving shelves. A large one at the bottom and two smaller ones at the top. But this is not the only way such shelves can be utilized. The shelves can be placed directly above each other, supported by center or side supports. Two, three or even more such shelves can be used, giving excellent service. Fig. 189 shows a turntable bearing fastened to a straight shelf with a circular shelf fastened to it. The size of such shelves must be

Handy Lazy Susan Kitchen Shelf
Figure 189

determined by the needs and the wishes of the person or persons that have them installed. Fig. 190 shows a rotating book rack. Such racks can be circular, some kind of polygon, or even oblong.

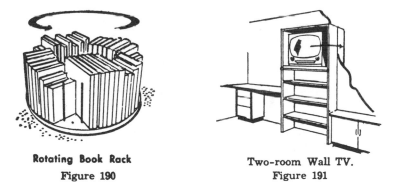

Rotating Book Rack
Figure 190

Two-room Wall TV.
Figure 191

Fig. 191 shows cabinets and shelves, combined with a two-room TV built into the wall between the two rooms. The TV is fastened to a turntable, so that it can be turned to face whichever room that is to receive the pictures. Fig. 192 shows revolving storage shelves for office or home. Here we have three circular shelves, supported by outside supports. Again, the shelves can be made larger or smaller than what is shown, and the number of the shelves can be increased or decreased. These

Storage shelves
for home or office
Figure 192

things must be determined by the needs of the owners. Fig. 193 shows a basement storage fixture that hangs from the ceiling, with shelves for hats, shoes and so forth.

Basement storage fixture.
Figure 193

The text and illustrations in this chapter furnished by
TRIANGLE MANUFACTURING COMPANY
700 Division Street
Oshkosh, Wisconsin
Note: This company manufactures bearings and swivels which are used to produce turntables and we would suggest that you write to them direct for any additional information regarding their products.

INDEX

INDEX